Staying Lean

Thriving, Not Just Surviving

Second Edition

Staying Lean

Thriving, Not Just Surviving

Second Edition

Peter Hines

Pauline Found

Gary Griffiths

Richard Harrison

CRC Press
Taylor & Francis Group
Boca Raton   London   New York

CRC Press is an imprint of the
Taylor & Francis Group, an **informa** business

A PRODUCTIVITY PRESS BOOK

First edition published by the Lean Enterprise Research Centre, Cardiff University, 2008. Second edition published by Productivity Press, New York, 2010.

Productivity Press
Taylor & Francis Group
270 Madison Avenue
New York, NY 10016

Printed in the United States of America on acid-free paper
10 9 8 7 6 5 4 3 2

International Standard Book Number: 978-1-4398-2617-1 (Paperback)

Visit the Taylor & Francis Web site at
http://www.taylorandfrancis.com

and the Productivity Press Web site at
http://www.productivitypress.com

Contents

List of Figures

Foreword

After having gone through many different improvement programs in several functional positions (from R&D through manufacturing engineering, production management, marketing, and sales to general management) since the start of my career in 1973, the need for an approach that puts all the pieces of the puzzle in the right place, in order to get to a balanced structure comprising a set of value creation activities that reinforce each other, without the sometimes seemingly unavoidable corrective action loops, became my very first priority and biggest professional desire.

Of course, I have implemented and experienced, like many others in industry, the benefits of all the wonderful and very promising improvement tools and so-called profit generators, like process re-engineering, kaizen, JIT, balanced scorecards, 5S, pull logistics, ERP systems, and many others that have provided generous levels of income to many consulting firms all over the world. But I have also experienced the fact that, on a stand-alone basis, these improvement activities have not provided the level of sustainable profitability for which I was looking.

Yes, I have sometimes seen rapid improvements and encouraging short- to sometimes medium-term results, but it simply didn't stay; ultimately and on top of that, there was a constant need for disproportional management attention and pressure.

Making all employees allies in the war against competition based on an unbeatable and transparently deployed strategy and clearly defined roles and responsibility throughout the company to realize profitable growth was what I have been seeking for quite some time.

In my first contacts with Professor Peter Hines at Cardiff University and Chris Butterworth at S A Partners, I became convinced that the holistic approach they had developed was the concept I had sought.

After having worked with them for many years now and seen the great successes we have achieved at Cogent Power, I am even more convinced that this is the way a business (any business—and not just automotive) should be run.

It is sheer excitement to get to a situation where the organization becomes truly self-propelling in exactly the direction that was defined in the company's strategy.

I hope that this book, which tells the story of implementing Lean Thinking in Cogent Power, will help you understand how effective this concept is.

Marcel Schabos
Cogent Power MD
2003–2007

Preface

The first edition of this publication was developed as part of the SUCCESS research program within the Cardiff University Innovative Manufacturing Research Centre (CUIMRC). The work was sponsored by the Engineering and Physical Science Research Council (EPSRC), Assa Abloy, Arvin Meritor, Complete Core Business Solutions, eBECS, Rizla, Royal Mint, Visteon, and Welsh Assembly Government. The Cardiff University Innovative Manufacturing Research Centre is a joint venture program involving colleagues from the Lean Enterprise Research Centre (LERC), Logistics Systems Dynamics Group (LSDG), and Manufacturing Engineering Centre (MEC).

The SUCCESS program was designed to extend the focus on Lean Thinking away from just "How do you get it going?" to "How do you sustain it over the medium to long term?" Within the research, this subject has been addressed at a range of scales from individuals to teams, factory shop floors and single plants to groups of companies, supply chains, and regions. This publication specifically addresses the group of companies' scale, a level that has attracted very little academic study. We believe sustaining change is more important for organizations than their first efforts in going Lean or using Lean to increase profits. Hence, this publication extends our earlier works on *Going Lean: A Guide to Implementation* and *Lean Profit Potential*.

The first edition of this publication was a winner of the Shingo Research and Professional Publication Prize Recipient for 2009. It covered how you can create a sustainable Lean business and Cogent Power's first two Lean Roadmaps along their journey. Since that time, the world has changed: Several members of Cogent Power's senior management team have moved on, steel prices have collapsed, and the "credit crunch" has created a sense of doom and gloom in the world economy. Set against this, we report on how Cogent Power has responded and worked through their third Lean Roadmap. This second updated edition includes these later developments.

Acknowledgments

The authors would like to thank a number of past and present people for their hard work and support within this publication. These include Nick Rich, Nicola Bateman, Jo Beale, Andrew Davies, Andrew Glanfield, Rebecca Travers, John Lucey, and many others of Cardiff University IMRC and LERC; and Ton Augustijn, Chris Brown, Bill Ford, Ron Harper, John Homewood, C-G Lenasson, Frans Liebreghts, Greg MacDougall, Peter Rose, Marcel Schabos, Todd Sheldan, Per Zettergren, and many others at Cogent Power. Thanks also go to Paul Allen, Chris Butterworth, Carmen Crocker, Kevin Eyre, Anthony Griffiths, Dave Lee, Phil Shelley, Kevin Wadge, and Leighton Williams of S A Partners. We would also like to thank the past co-authors David Taylor, Riccardo Silvi, and Monica Bartolini as well as Chris Craycraft from Whirlpool.

EPSRC Grant GR/375505/01 is gratefully acknowledged.

Professor Peter Hines, Dr. Pauline Found,
Gary Griffiths, and Richard Harrison

About the Authors

Professor Peter Hines held the chair in supply chain management at Cardiff University's Lean Enterprise Research Centre until 2010 and is the chairman of S A Partners as well as an adjunct professor in Lean Enterprise at the University of South Australia. He followed a successful career in the distribution and manufacturing industry before joining Cardiff Business School in 1992, and his work on extending the boundaries of Lean thinking has received international, widespread attention. He has written or co-written more than fifty books and papers, including *Going Lean* (2000) and *Lean Profit Potential* (2002). He is an editorial adviser for five journals, including the *International Journal of Logistics: Research and Applications*, which he started, and is a skilled Lean mentor and coach, especially within multi-site operations, strategy deployment, and supply chain management.

Dr Pauline Found is a fellow of the Institute of Operations Management and holds a diploma in Environmental Management, B.A., B.Sc., MBA, and Ph.D. She is employed as a senior research associate at Cardiff University. Pauline was a researcher on the SUCCESS program at Cardiff University Innovative Manufacturing Research Centre (IMRC) that conducted the research into sustainability of Lean implementations. Prior to joining Cardiff University in 2004, Pauline had a successful career in industry for fifteen years, working for major UK FTSE 100 organizations, gaining management experience in purchasing, operations planning, quality, and human resource management. In addition to co-authoring *Staying Lean: Thriving Not Just Surviving*, she has published several papers on Lean and organizational change, and has presented the findings at major international conferences and industrial workshops. In 2009 she was elected to serve as president of the College of Behavior in Operations Management, a college of the Production and Operations Management Society (POMS), an international professional organization representing the interests of POM professionals from around the world.

Gary Griffiths has an industrial engineering background with more than twenty years of hands-on experience in continuous improvement and Lean thinking. Combining practice with research throughout his career, he graduated to the master's degree level in 2000 from the University of Wales. Gary has been with S A Partners since 2003 and has proven credibility in designing multi-site, integrated continuous improvement programs for a range of corporate clients (Gary was, in fact, the Lean program manager for the Cogent work). Having successfully applied the practices and principles of Lean in order creation, order fulfillment, and innovation business processes, Gary has worked in a range of business sectors, including FMCG, engineering, health and automotive, and has covered every continent in the world in doing so. Gary is head of capability development at S A Partners and specializes in lean diagnostics and implementation, Lean maturity roadmap design, equipment effectiveness, and Lean leadership. Gary currently teaches Lean leadership at the University of South Australia.

Richard Harrison joined the Mars confectionery group straight out of school and, following completion of a business degree and a two-year post-graduate sponsorship at the London Business School, gained broad experience working at board level in sales and marketing roles with premium branded products across a range of different industries. Richard joined S A Partners in 2002 with the assignment to take Lean off the shop floor and apply the philosophy within the sales and marketing environment. He is currently a managing consultant and a specialist in customer value and sales performance improvement and brings a wealth of practical experience to clients from across a wide variety of global market sectors and industries, including consumer products, retail, engineering, manufacturing, food, packaging, software, aerospace, automotive, medical, pharmaceutical, insurance, finance, the public sector, and legal. Within S A Partners he heads up the product group development for customer value and sales. Richard is a Master Practitioner in NLP.

THE JOURNEY TO LEAN

Over the past fifteen years, we have consistently been asked a series of searching questions about the application of Lean Thinking:

- Where do I start?
- Is there a road map that I can follow?
- What does Lean Thinking involve?
- Who will I have to involve?
- Is it only applicable to the shop floor?
- Is it only for manufacturing firms?
- What will the benefits be?
- Will it make me more profitable?

To answer these questions, we have produced two previous publications, *Going Lean* and *Lean Profit Potential*, which give practical insight into these topics. However, because these publications were produced in the early 2000s, the set of questions we are asked has widened, with a series of additional queries:

- How long is it before the benefits start fading away?
- Why do people seem to have lost their enthusiasm for Lean here?
- What is the secret of sustainability?
- What is the difference between managing and leading a Lean change?
- How do we ensure continued buy-in from the workforce?

We have written this book to help you answer these questions and ensure that you don't just start a successful Lean program in your business but that you sustain and build on your early successes. We have included a range of sources of further information and a jargonbuster toward the end. Throughout this book we use a real case, that of Cogent Power, to illustrate how Lean can be applied in a sustainable way across a group company operating mostly from brownfield sites within a range of product categories, countries, and cultures.

We hope you enjoy reading the book and wish you a sustainable Lean journey.

Chapter 1

Lean Vision and Principles

The characteristics of the Lean organization and the Lean supply chain are described in *Lean Thinking – Banish Waste and Create Wealth in Your Corporation* by Jim Womack and Dan Jones. This book provides a vision of a world transformed from mass production to a Lean enterprise. The authors highlight the huge amounts of waste that occur in most organizations and show that a systematic attack on waste, both within companies and along the supply chains, can have tremendous benefits to the short-run profitability and long-term prospects of companies and organizations. Lean production methods were pioneered by Toyota in Japan. *Lean Thinking* distills the essence of the Lean approach into five key principles and shows how the concepts can be extended beyond automotive production to any company or organization, in any sector, in any country.

The Five Lean Principles

1. Specify what does and does not create value from the customer's perspective and not from the perspectives of individual firms, functions, and departments.
2. Identify all the steps necessary to design, order, and produce the product across the whole value stream to highlight non-value-adding waste.
3. Make those actions that create value flow without interruption, detours, backflows, waiting, or scrap.
4. Only make what is pulled by the customer.
5. Strive for perfection by continually removing successive layers of waste as they are uncovered.

These principles are fundamental to the elimination of waste. They are easy to remember (although not always easy to achieve!) and should be the guide for everyone

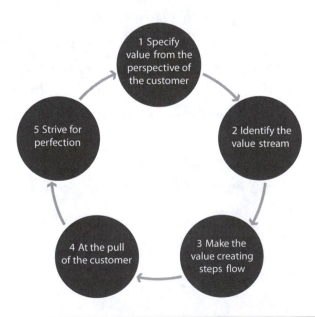

Figure S.1.1   The five Lean principles.

in the organization who becomes involved in the Lean transformation. If you are serious about implementing a sustainable Lean system, then the people in your organization need to read *Lean Thinking* at the outset. If they do not have enough time to do that, they probably won't implement Lean and certainly won't sustain it!

Understanding Value and Waste

To go Lean and stay Lean, you continually need to understand customers and what they value. To get your organization focused on these needs, you must define the value streams or processes inside your company and, later, the value streams or processes in your wider supply chain as well. To satisfy customers, you will need to eliminate or at least reduce the wasteful activities for which your customers would not wish to pay.

Next, you must find ways of

■ Setting the direction
■ Fixing targets
■ Seeing whether or not change is actually occurring

You need a framework to deliver value for your customers, as well as a toolkit to make the change. The steps required to go Lean are described in *Going Lean* and *Lean Profit Potential*.

Lean focuses on creating value for the customer. This means eliminating, or at least reducing, everything else. To do this, Lean leader Toyota identified three key areas to address: *muda, mura,* and *muri*. Organizations that implement, but often fail to sustain Lean systems, usually only concentrate on *muda*.

Muda (Waste)

Identifying and eliminating waste is fundamental to a Lean organization. However, on its own, it is rarely sufficient. Improved customer focus and productivity gains lead to leaner operations, which in turn help to expose further waste and quality problems in the system. The systematic attack on waste is also a systematic assault on the factors underlying poor quality and fundamental management problems.

> **Readers beware!**
> Many organizations fail to recognize the importance of *mura* and *muri*. Pay attention to all three—*muda, mura, and muri*—if you want to succeed in and sustain your Lean implementation.

Waste is anything that does not add value to the customer. As a guide, seven wastes were identified by Shigeo Shingo as part of the Toyota Production System. The Japanese call this *muda*. Use the chart in Table 1.1 to make a note of any of these wastes in your business.

Mura (Unevenness)

Once Lean practitioners understand what *muda* is, they can focus on *mura*. *Mura* translates as unevenness or variability. If you have ever had a discussion with Six

Table 1.1   Wastes in your organization.

Waste	Description	Examples in your organization
1 Overproduction	Producing too much or too soon, resulting in poor flow of information or goods and excess inventory.	
2 Defects	Frequent errors in paperwork, product quality problems, or poor delivery performance.	
3 Unnecessary inventory	Excessive storage and delay of information or products, resulting in excessive cost and poor customer service.	
4 Inappropriate processing	Going about work processes using the wrong set of tools, procedures or systems, often when a simpler approach may be more effective.	
5 Excessive transportation	Excessive movement of people, information or goods resulting in wasted time, effort, and cost.	
6 Waiting	Long periods of inactivity for people, information or goods, resulting in poor flow and long lead times.	
7 Unnecessary motion	Poor workplace organization, resulting in poor ergonomics, e.g., excessive bending or stretching and frequently lost items.	

Sigma devotees, this is probably what they were talking about when they tried to describe their approach. This may well have led to a debate about whether to use implementation tools from Lean (reducing waste) or Six Sigma (reducing unevenness). You may even have had that debate yourself. Well, the reality is that you need both sets (see the later section on "Technology, Tools, and Techniques"). Consider Figure 1.1; it shows the order intake of a manufacturing firm and its response time that was not regarded as good by its customers. Should we reduce the lead-time or reduce the variation?

Simple use of the "5 Whys" (keep asking "Why?" to a problem until you have the root cause) will yield the answer. In many cases you will find that the *muda* is being caused by the *mura*. Here, the variability of demand is caused by the way salespeople are rewarded. This in turn causes a long lead-time. Trying to sort out this long lead-time without addressing the reward system would be as effective as rearranging the deck chairs on the Titanic. Hence, always look for *mura* as well as *muda*.

Muri (Overburden)

Have you ever tried to introduce Lean into an office environment where they do not actually make things? Did you start the discussion by describing waste? Did you define waste as everything the customer does not want to pay for? Did you describe this as everything that was not concerned with the physical transformation of the product? Did they get the idea that everything they did was waste? Did you find it hard to embed Lean? Did they view Lean as a way to reduce jobs? If so, what was missing was an attention to *muri*. In our recent work at Cardiff University, we have started to apply Lean to ourselves. To do this we have adopted the motto "lightening the load." We start our interventions (which are all in-office-type

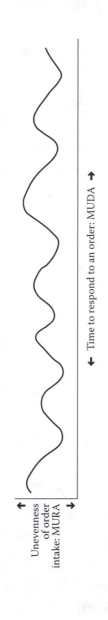

Figure 1.1   Unevenness of orders (MURA) and time to respond (MUDA).

environments because we do not actually make things) with a question such as, "In your daily job are there any things that frustrate you or lead to you doing too much work or doing the same thing many times?" We have yet to receive a short answer!

However, the reason for the *muri* is often due to unevenness. So why, for example, do nearly all post-graduate courses start in September at the same time as undergraduate courses, causing a huge spike in work for admissions staff? Well, they always have.

So, as shown in Figure 1.2, *mura* leads to *muri*, which probably leads to too many admissions staff for the remainder of the year (*muda*). We are sure you can find many examples in your organization of these vicious circles. The key point is that we all need to look for *muda*, *mura*, and *muri*. However, the most engaging and least threatening of these is *muri*; and sadly for the sustainability of Lean transformations, it is the one least often mentioned or addressed.

Going Lean and Staying Lean

So why do Lean programs not sustain? Well, there may be many reasons but nearly all will have something to do with people, their leadership, and their engagement. This is often made worse by a preoccupation with Lean and Six Sigma implementation tools. Take, for example, white goods manufacturer Whirlpool and its application of Lean a few years ago in its North American facilities. The company adopted a Lean approach across its dozen sites with two distinctly

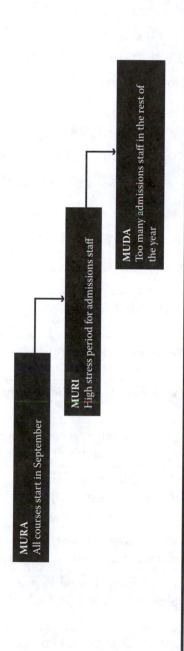

Figure 1.2 MUDA, MURI, and MURA in the admission of students at UK universities.

different approaches (Figure 1.3). At half of the sites, they adopted a highly focused Kaizen Blitz approach on the shop floor that yielded rapid results. At the other sites, they adopted a much more careful but systematic approach focusing on culture change. In the short term, this yielded little; but in the long term, it flourished—while the early "hero story" sites using Kaizen Blitz started to fail.

So what are the secrets of this "green line" sustainability? Well, many of them are summarized in Table 1.2; use this table to see how well you are doing.

Table 1.2   Ten tips for staying lean; how are you doing?

		Ten Tips for Staying Lean	*How Are You Doing?*
	1.	Think of Lean as a philosophy for success rather than a series of tools and techniques.	
	2.	Apply lean right across the organization, not just in the parts the textbooks talk about.	
	3.	Focus on improving processes or value streams not departments.	
	4.	Link everything you do to creating value for your customers, your organization, and your people.	
	5.	Don't just copy others, think through your approach based on what you are trying to achieve.	
	6.	Make everyone aware of what you are trying to achieve and why you are doing that.	
	7.	Align your communication and key performance measures to creating and sustaining a lean organization.	
	8.	Provide sufficient resources in terms of people and training right across the organization, not just your lean coaches.	

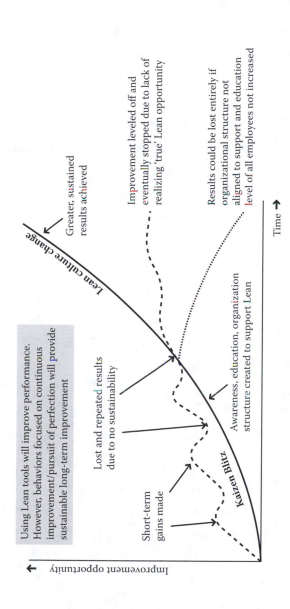

Figure 1.3 Route to performance improvement over time (*Source:* Chris Craycroft, Whirlpool).

Thinking It Through

In our academic ivory tower we have attempted to think through what you need to do. Applying Lean is best explained by an analogy to an iceberg. It is not what you see, but rather it is generally what you do not see that is more important…back to the Titanic again!

So, what did we see on our Japanese Lean pilgrimages at the end of the previous century? We went to a series of manufacturing firms that made discrete products from a series of components, such as cars or electronics equipment. Within these firms we went to where the action was: the shop floors. What we saw was marvelous: We saw 5S (*seiri, seiton, seiso, seiketsu*, and *shitsuke*), we saw kanban, we saw total productive maintenance (TPM), we saw flow, and we saw all the typical Lean tools and techniques that you read about in textbooks, good examples of which are *The New Lean Toolbox* by John Bicheno and *Lean Toolbox: Essential Guide to Transformation (4th edition)* by John Bicheno and Matthias Holweg.

With a little further gentle probing, we also managed to establish that the secret to these firms' successes was that they worked in overriding processes. Inside the factory these were often described as Quality, Cost, and Delivery. We deciphered these as three key internal processes:

1. Innovation of new products (Quality)
2. Life-cycle management of costs (Cost)
3. Order fulfillment of existing products to existing customers (Delivery)

In addition to these tools and techniques, and process-based management, it was what we did not see that was probably more important. In the Lean Sustainability Iceberg Model, there are three key areas under the water that are all people related.

The Sustainable Lean Iceberg

Figure 1.4 illustrates the sustainable Lean iceberg model. The sustainable Lean thinker needs to learn to see and act below the waterline as well as above it. The items below the waterline include strategy and alignment, leadership, and behavior and engagement.

Strategy and Alignment

Many businesses we come across fail to establish a coherent strategy, vision, and purpose. However, even if you in your organization do, this is not enough in itself. What you need is a strategy that is fully communicated and deployed throughout the organization. It needs to describe

- **What** you want to do and,
- **Why** this is important. This will guide your staff in
- **How** to focus their change activity.

We offer two questions to test whether this is the case today:

1. Can all the people in your organization clearly articulate what your strategy is?

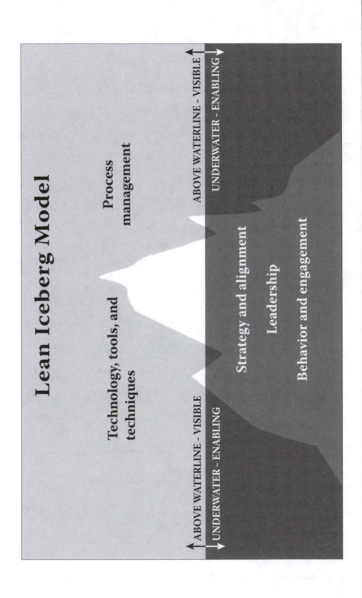

Figure 1.4 The Sustainable Lean Iceberg model.

2. Can they demonstrate what they are doing themselves in their normal job to help the organization achieve this strategy?

If your answers are not clear, you need to pay greater attention to strategy and alignment. In our experience, in a typical organization, no more than 20 percent of staff can articulate the strategy, and no more than 20 percent of these are able to show how they are directly contributing. This may mean that less than 5 percent of people are directly contributing to effective change.

Leadership

The second "below the waterline" element is leadership. Many organizations possess good managers but not necessarily good leaders. Leaders are usually characterized as having a guiding vision, passion, and integrity. When leading change, they must have high energy levels, be innovative, focus on people, inspire trust, have a long-range perspective, and challenge the status quo.

The role of the leader is to inspire with words, deeds, and actions. This involves allowing everyone in the organization to take part in the strategy process and encouraging everyone to get involved in delivering the actual change and reducing fire-fighting and non-value-adding work. A leader inspires his or her organization to change from a typical organization to a sustainable one.

Which of the two types of organization, shown here as Figure 1.5 and Figure 1.6, has your leadership inspired? If it is the first (Figure 1.5), then unless you address your

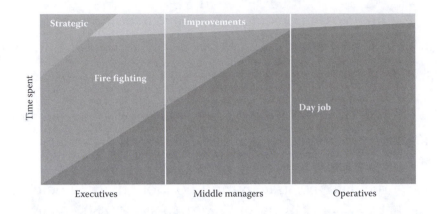

Figure 1.5 The typical organization.

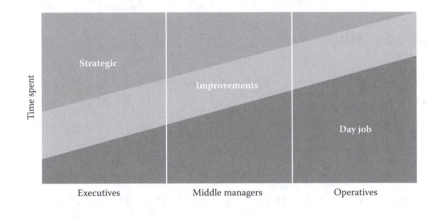

Figure 1.6 The sustainable organization.

job design structure at all levels, it will be next to impossible to create a sustainable Lean business.

Behavior and Engagement

The engagement of people on a Lean journey is essential. It will predict their behavior and your ultimate success. There are many steps on the engagement journey as you can see below, but effective strategy, alignment, and leadership are a good start. Other key elements are partly due to the characteristics of the individuals themselves, how they are communicated with, and how they are trained. The general social norms of your organization will also have an impact on the journey as you progress from acceptance to commitment, as shown in Figure 1.7.

Use Table 1.3 to check your own personal engagement. What about your colleagues? How engaged are they?

In summary, to establish a sustainable Lean organization, you need to address each of the five elements illustrated in our Lean sustainability iceberg:

Table 1.3   Check your own personal engagement.

Engagement area	Strongly disagree	Disagree	Neither agree nor disagree	Agree	Strongly agree
I enjoy my job and am clear of what is expected of me.					
My job gives me a strong sense of achievement.					
I am clear what I need to do to improve.					
I am keen to make improvements.					
I enjoy working with my colleagues.					
My working environment is pleasant.					

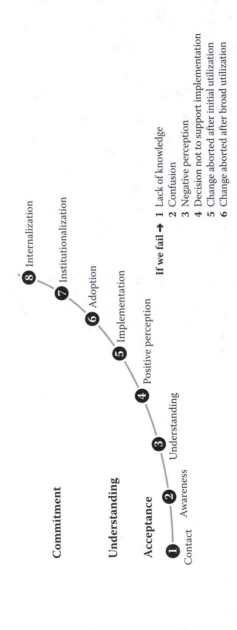

Figure 1.7   Stages of a Lean journey (*Source:* Chris Craycroft, Whirlpool).

1. Strategy and alignment
2. Leadership
3. Behavior and engagement
4. Process management
5. Technology, tools, and techniques

This should be achieved at all levels of the organization, not just on the shop floor. When we tried to find texts on what to do right across an organization, we were hugely disappointed. We found almost no guidance on how to do this more widely than at a single location site, so we decided to provide this guide on how to apply your own Lean iceberg at a group company level. In Chapter 2 we describe our case company.

Company Background

Cogent Power began implementing Lean in 2003 to improve its competitiveness in the marketplace and help turn around its financial performance. Now some years down the road, the company has transformed its approach, with a renewed customer focus that has led to *exponential sales growth* and a *culture of continuous improvement*.

The Road to Lean

Electrical steels play an essential role in the generation, transmission, distribution, and use of electrical power, and they are one of the most important magnetic materials produced today. Global electrical steel manufacturer Cogent Power has its head office in the United Kingdom and operates out of three major plants (in the United Kingdom, Sweden, and Canada) that function as semi-autonomous business units. Each operating plant has its own management structure, and commercial and financial responsibilities. An internal supply chain exists wherein the UK plant supplies the Canadian plant with some of the raw materials for further processing and conversion.

This is shown by the pale gray highlighting in Figure 2.1 and is where Cogent Power focused its initial activities.

Company History

The union of the three plants occurred as a result of all being owned, or incorporated into, European Electrical Steels in 1991. Prior to this point they had unique and individual company histories. European Electrical Steels (EES) Ltd. resulted from a joint venture in 1991 between British Steel, which owned the UK plants, and Svenskt Stål AB (SSAB), which owned the Swedish and North American plants.

In 2000, EES, now part of the newly formed Corus Group Plc, acquired the Kienle + Spiess Group, companies that specialized in downstream processing of non-oriented electrical steel. Cogent Power Ltd. was formed as a joint venture out of this acquisition and comprised plants in the United Kingdom, Sweden, North America, Germany, and Hungary. Subsequently, Cogent Power sold the downstream businesses and these have returned to private ownership. In 2006, the Cogent Group comprised plants in the United Kingdom, Sweden, and Canada, with its head office in the United Kingdom.

The Canadian plant only began operation in 1970, but both the UK and Swedish plants have much longer and varied histories dating back to the nineteenth and sixteenth centuries, respectively.

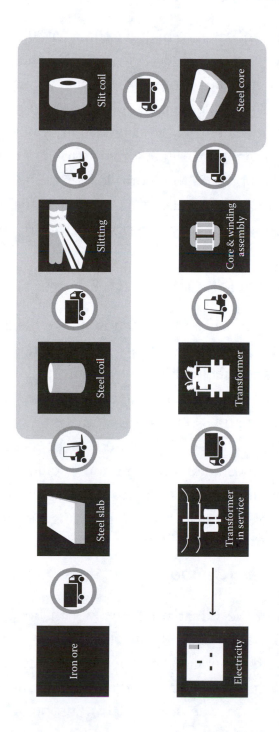

Figure 2.1 Cogent Power supply chain 2003.

Cogent Power (UK) Ltd.

Electrical steel has been manufactured at the United Kingdom site in South Wales since 1898 when it was founded by a private company. Before World War I, more than 3,000 people were employed at this site; with the advent of new technology, approximately 400 people now produce more than 186,000 metric tons of electrical steel a year. The plant is the world leader in the production of grain-oriented steel that is used in transformers. Table 2.1 shows the history of Cogent Power (UK) Ltd.

Cogent Power (Sweden) A.B.

The Swedish plant has a history, shown in Table 2.2, dating back to the sixteenth century that covers railways, automotives, and steelmaking. Originally the company was completely vertically integrated and owned iron ore mines with iron- and steel-making plants.

Since the 1980s, these have closed, or been sold, and now the plant concentrates on non-grain-oriented steel and produces more than 100,000 metric tons of electrical steel for use in motors and generators, employing 235 people.

Cogent Power (Canada) Inc.

In comparison, the Canadian plant, which began operating in 1970, has a relatively short history. It formed as part of a North American and Mexican group of steelmakers servicing the Canadian and U.S. transformer market. The group was acquired by European companies and eventually became part of EES. Later, with the

Table 2.1   Company history, Orb Steelworks, UK.

Cogent Power (UK) Ltd – A Brief History	
• **1898** WR Lysaghts company starts at Orb Works. • **1906** Transporter bridge built to carry men to work. • **1913** Expansion to 40 hand-worked hot mills, 6 steam-driven engines, 3,000 employees. • **1914 – 1915** Diversification into products for Great War effort: trench plate, helmet steel. • **1920** GKN acquires controlling interest. • **1933** UK first mechanical rolling mill installed. • **1939 – 1945** Diversification again to help war effort: corrugated sheets and sheet steel. Pioneering rolling of "duralumin" for aircraft. • **1944** King George VI and Queen Elizabeth visit the works in recognition of war effort. • **1947 – 1950** GKN and Lysaghts join, founding the Steel Company of Wales: electrical steels production for global customers begins. • **1965** Last hand mills phased out. • **1967** Orb becomes part of British Steel Corporation. • **1989** British Steel Corporation privatised.	• **1991** Orb becomes Orb Electrical Steels Ltd., part of European Electrical Steels Ltd. • **1995** Orb becomes Accredited Investor in People. • **1996** Orb receives Queen's Award for Export Achievement. • **1998** Orb celebrates centenary with Open Day. • **2000** EES acquires Keinle & Spiess group and forms Cogent Power Ltd. • **2002** Orb re-accredited as an Investor in People. • **2003** Adopted Lean Thinking as the cornerstone of its forward business and operational strategy • **2004** The Lean Thinking Philosophy became embedded as the Lean Lifestyle with aesthetic business improvements and operational/financial benefits. • **2006** Cogent Power sold its downstream business and the Cogent Group comprised Orb, Surahammars Bruk, and Cogent Power Inc. consolidated in Canada.

Cogent Power in Sweden – A Brief History

16th century	A "Crown hammer" in Surahammar
1627	Chancellor Axel Oxenstierna acquires two estates in Surahammar and erects a hammer at the weir
1845	The goldsmith E.A. Zethelius buys the works and initiates the expansion
1866	The production of railway wheels for Swedish State Railways starts
1897	The first Swedish car is made in Surahammar
1916	ASEA acquires Surahammars Bruk
1917	First delivery of hot rolled electrical steel
1959	Production of cold rolled oriented electrical steel starts
1974	New blast furnace and Q-BOP steelmaking
1981	Mining, ironmaking, and steelmaking are closed down
1984	The North American companies are acquired
1986	Svenskt Stål AB (SSAB) buys Surahammars Bruk
1991	Surahammars Bruk is incorporated into European Electrical Steels Ltd EES, a joint venture between British Stell (75%) and SSAB (25%)
1993	Production of gain/oriented ends. Capacity for non-oriented steel is doubled
1995	New yearly production record; more than 100K tonnes produced
2000	EES buys Kienle+Spiess
2001	Cogent Power Ltd. is formed

Table 2.2 Company history of Surahammars, Sweden.

purchase of Kienle + Spiess, it became Cogent Power Inc. In 2003, following major restructuring, the North American operations were centralized and all production was consolidated and moved to a new state-of-the-art plant in Ontario.

Cogent Power in Canada warehouses and slits a full range of electrical sheets for the transformer industry. It also provides a wide range of wound and stacked cores (included assembled) for small and medium power transformers.

The Challenge Facing Cogent

In 2003, the company was facing a number of challenges:

- Substantial pre-tax losses from global operations
- Business was losing cash from a number of its operating plants
- Static order book with emphasis on lower-margin products

To meet these challenges, a new managing director, Marcel, was appointed to lead the business turnaround. He put in place a new organizational structure (Figure 2.2), based on a head office in the United Kingdom and three operating divisions: electrical steels, laminations, and transformers. In 2006, the Laminations Division was sold and the new structure, based on electrical steels and transformers, produced across three sites in the United Kingdom, Sweden, and Canada, was established.

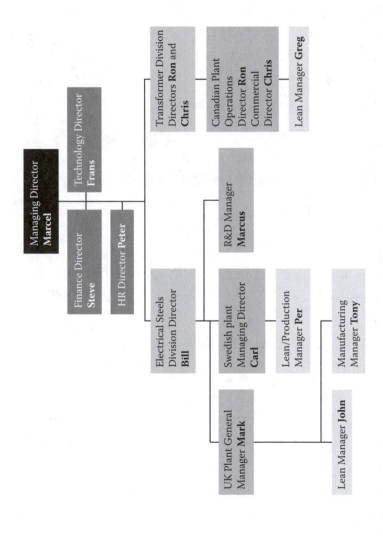

Figure 2.2 Cogent Power organization structure 2003–2006.

When Marcel took over in 2003, the culture and philosophy of the company, despite national differences, was based on traditional steel manufacturing. The main operational key performance indicator (KPI) was metric tons of output produced, driving a mindset and culture of machine and labor efficiency. As a result, there were high levels of inventory but poor levels of delivery performance. High levels of inventory and long batch runs were making the plants unable to respond quickly to changes in demand. It was Marcel's role to turn around the company's financial performance. He knew that to do this, he needed to turn the company into a *Lean enterprise*. Over the next few pages we follow what happened.

II

BELOW THE WATERLINE

In the next two sections, we examine the iceberg in detail, using Cogent Power as an illustration, but we will return later to reflect on its journey and the lessons learned.

Beneath the waterline are those enabling features that support a Lean transformation, strategy and alignment, leadership, and employee behavior and engagement. This section examines the features that can be found below the waterline of a "real" Lean company.

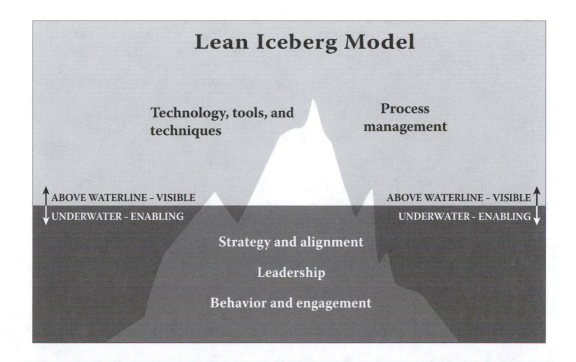

Figure S.2.1   The Sustainable Lean Iceberg Model.

Chapter 3

Strategy and Alignment

A successful strategy usually begins with:

- A realistic assessment of the current situation
- A coherent vision of the future
- An understanding of the transition required to bridge from the present to the future

At the heart of the Toyota Production System (or what Toyota now terms the "Thinking People System") is *Hoshin Kanri*, the "Shining Needle." This is described in detail in *Beyond Strategic Vision: Effective Corporate Action with Hoshin Planning* by Cowley and Domb. In Japan, *Hoshin Kanri* is the term for directional management, or directional control. It is the means for setting the direction for the organization; hence the "shining needle," the needle in a compass. *Hoshin Kanri* is also known by its Western name of "policy deployment," which was introduced in our earlier books, *Going Lean* and *Lean Profit Potential*. We use the term "policy deployment" but we are not distinguishing it from *Hoshin Kanri* in any way.

Policy deployment is really a strategic management system that shares the vision and goals for the business with everyone in the organization. It gives senior management clarity of purpose and engages everyone in the priorities of the organization, giving employees an element of ownership and a sense of control. However, of all the Japanese management systems, policy deployment is the most invisible and most difficult to copy. See *Value Stream Management* by Hines, Lamming, Jones, Cousins, and Rich for more information on policy deployment.

> There should be a relationship between you and your colleagues and you should both be looking in the same direction. If you're looking in different directions, you will never be successful.
> —Frans, Technology Director

Why is strategy and alignment fundamental to sustaining Lean? Well, *strategy* is about improvement and setting the direction for the organization. *Alignment* is making sure that everybody understands the strategy, and that everything they do contributes to the success of achieving the organizational goals. The best way of checking this is to see how the organization measures and monitors progress using Key Performance Indicators (KPIs). We believe that there must always be a link between the KPIs, the strategy, and the Lean improvement projects. KPIs that are not linked directly to business goals take away valuable resources, and this is a waste. So it is very important that the KPIs are clearly aligned with the overall goals and that they drive the right behaviors.

To gain commitment and ownership, employees need to feel involved in setting the KPIs so that they are clear about their own part in the overall scheme; if everyone shares in the vision and can see how it all fits together, they will understand the importance of meeting their own targets. Measuring and monitoring effective KPIs ensure that the business stays on course and that the improvement program is sustained over time.

Cogent Power uses "business cockpits" to deploy and sustain the management process. The business cockpit is a visual management system to display, on a single A3 page (11 x 17 inches), everything that is important to help run the business. This should be applied in each area of the business, not just on the shop floor, and may include issues, improvement project plans, performance measures, and key financial reports. There are business cockpits at all levels of the organization, starting at the strategic top level and cascading down through the organization to the operational team level; everyone is represented on one or more business cockpits. The business cockpits become the focus of regular review meetings as they hold all the information necessary to monitor progress and take corrective action. When we spoke to managers at Cogent Power, they told us their cockpits drive the business at all levels, not some dusty annual plan only known by a few senior managers.

There are different cockpits at different levels. At the top level are the corporate strategic issues and company measures and targets (Figure 3.1); these measures are cascaded downward as process, functional or team targets, and measures. Each of these has its own cockpit so that managers can easily see how things are progressing

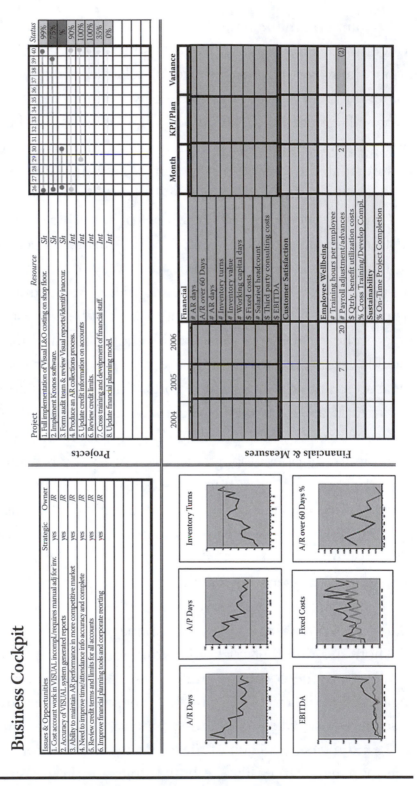

Figure 3.1   Cogent Power business cockpit.

in their area of responsibility. Managers and teams were encouraged to define and set their own targets and measures, as long as they were aligned and contributing to the overall business strategy and objectives.

> We didn't tell the businesses how to define the KPIs, and we told them that they could change them as often as they wanted, because the only objective of a KPI is to give you feedback on the quality of your performance.
>
> —Marcel, Managing Director

In the illustration in Figure 3.2, the business-level cockpit shows top-level business performance measures. The operations department cockpit includes measures for overall production performance, typically including OEE (Overall Equipment Effectiveness), OTIF (On-Time In Full), direct costs, etc. These are referred to in Cogent Power as "Line of Sight" boards.

Cascading the Strategy into the Business

Each team has more detail on their cockpit of the OEE by machine, or bottleneck process, and the improvement project team will have measures on improvement targets and project progress. The cockpits have all the information that the team leaders need to manage their sections, functional (or process) managers need to manage their departments, and senior managers need to manage the business; and each has a clear link, or "Line of Sight," to the other (Figure 3.3). The cockpits are reviewed and updated regularly. Senior management formally reviews

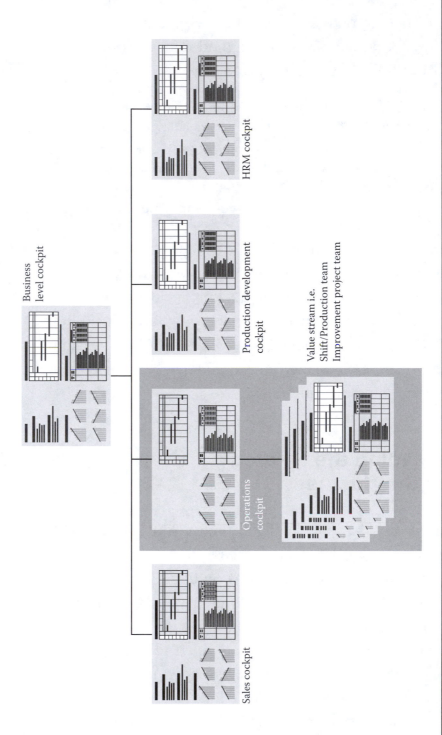

Figure 3.2 Cascading the strategy into the business (strategy deployment and alignment).

	Euro-Strategy	Return to Profit	Performance Improvements	Lean Implementation
QA	New QA office inclusive Lab/QA/QC	Implementation of new CAR/Returns database	Intro of Six Sigma for QC Job ownership for line setters	Intro of SOPs at the stamping station 5S QA Dept
IT	Ensure IT and comms services available in restructured plants	Value for money approach for service, etc. Develop systems to reduce costs	Introduction of production planning and Rhombus systems	Support system changes to reduce waste OTIF reporting
SALES	Relocation of Bilston sales office, 5S of files, more customer communication	Identify sales projects with added value (shaft insertion, machined cores, etc.)	Currently fire fighting; once dust settles hope to find time to actively address sales KPI	5S Sales KPIs
HR	Leadership development (adoption of Corus model) to help develop skills	Flexible manpower strategies, responsive in employee relations/ development	Reward system to effectively support and drive growth and performance	Best HR effective and efficient by introducing KPIs

Figure 3.3 Line of sight from business-level strategic objectives to team objectives.

the business-level cockpit every month. Process or functional and team cockpits are reviewed weekly or monthly, depending on the nature of the KPIs and workplans. Operational targets are reviewed on a daily or shift basis, and these are available to the entire workforce.

So how do you go about policy deployment? The foundation of policy deployment is Deming's scientific method—plan, do, check, act (PDCA), at every level, but always aligned to the core business strategy (Figure 3.4).

P: Planning

Planning defines and sets the strategy. Strategy is about direction and vision, deciding where you want to go, what you need to do to get there, and who you need to take you there. Strategy is also about getting the right organizational model and having the right people in place to support you. Strategy is sometimes about making hard decisions on the best management model to apply. This

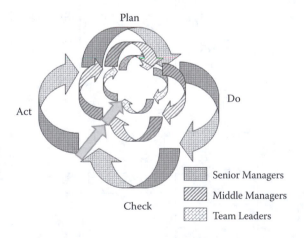

Figure 3.4   Deming's principle of PDCA at different levels in an organization.

is because it is important that the organizational structure and management team are capable of delivering the strategy and that they all are aligned toward the same common goals. You will hear more about this in the leadership and behaviors chapters.

> You have to make sure that it is the right organizational model and that these are the right people. If they are not the right people, it doesn't mean that Lean is not right. It is important to evaluate and assess the organization as a model and ask if the people are willing to change.
> —Frans, Technology Director, Cogent Power Group

Strategy is about a vision for the future; but in order to get there, you need to know where you are at the moment, what the gaps are between the current state and the future state, and what factors you need to address to reach your goal. You tackle this by starting at the beginning, and by understanding the external factors that are affecting your business right now and those that you predict will affect you in the future. Some organizations use a PEST (political, economic, social, and technological) analysis for this. PEST can also be extended to include environmental and legal issues (PESTEL). PEST assesses the market or industry from the company perspective. Once you have defined the external factors, you need to do the same for the internal factors. It is important to make a complete and honest appraisal of everything that is affecting the organization now, and of factors that are likely to affect it in the future. The next step is to perform an analysis of the business strengths, weaknesses, opportunities, and threats; this is known as a

SWOT analysis. SWOT measures a business unit or idea; PEST measures the market or the industry. You always do PEST before SWOT.

Figure 3.5 is an example of Cogent Power's early SWOT analysis; it is something you could try for your organization. It is usually best done as a group so that you can discuss the items. You might find that it is easier to define the weaknesses and threats rather than the strengths and opportunities, but a well-constructed SWOT or TOWS analysis can be a very useful tool for understanding situations and making decisions.

Strengths	Weaknesses
No. 1 in Europe	High cost structure
Presence in Eastern Europe	Cash drain
Expertise	No market strategy
Wide product range	Poor forecasting
New management structure	Poor process capability
Brand image	Limited sharing of technology
Customer loyalty	Lack of innovation
Opportunities	**Threats**
Increase added value business	Cash drain
Lean thinking to improve process capability	Increased competition
Increase automotive business	Customer migration
Share technology	Engineering skills shortage
Outsourcing opportunities	Customer consolidation
	Increased customer requirements

Figure 3.5 Cogent Power's SWOT (strengths, weaknesses, opportunities, threats) analysis.

A technique used at Cogent Power is known as a Linked SWOT or TOWS analysis (Figure 3.6). This makes a linkage between the external market opportunities and threats and the organization's strengths and weaknesses. Linked SWOTs make it easy to see where effort needs to be focused and to decide which issues need to be addressed.

The "zone of riches" is where the company has existing strengths and there are market opportunities that can be exploited. The "wannabe zone" is where there are market opportunities, but the company is currently weak. It makes sense here to develop capabilities, turning weakness into strength. Where there are market threats, now or in the future, the zones are referred to as the "hazard zone" or the "get tough zone." In these zones, the organization may choose to leverage strength to repel competition. Where the company is weak, it may choose to outsource or even exit the market completely.

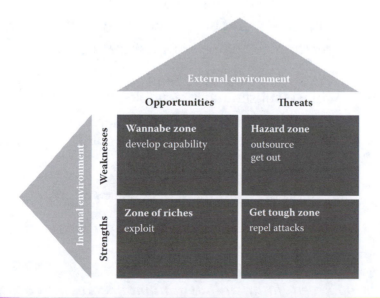

Figure 3.6   Linked SWOT, or TOWS analysis framework.

This was a major exercise at Cogent Power, involving all the senior managers. From the analysis, eight to ten critical success factors (CSFs) were negotiated and selected. For a large company or group of companies, the process would need to be repeated at each business unit. It should always start at the corporate level, to set the overall direction and business goals, but should then be repeated at each level to identify the business unit CSFs needed to achieve the overall corporate strategy. At Cogent Power, this was developed at the group level, then repeated at divisional and business unit levels, and then cascaded down to the teams. The CSFs formed the basis of the organizational and operational strategies.

The example shown here reveals how the divisional CSFs are translated to strategic business units (SBUs) and finally to the sales team.

1. Divisional-level CSFs:
    - Exceed shareholder financial targets.
    - Significantly reduce total transformation cost structure to gain competitive advantage and enable outsourcing.
    - Achieve substantial/profitable sales growth.
    - Understand and deliver customer value.
    - Attract, develop, and retain flexible, motivated, and service-oriented workforce.
    - Develop new products or services aligned to market needs.

2. Divisional CSFs translated to SBU:
    - *Exceed financial commitments to shareholders for 2006 relating to working capital management*

and cash, and earnings before interest, taxes, depreciation, and amortization (EBITDA). We will be challenged in 2006 with working capital and cash management with the change of supply. As a result, our inventory turns must be much higher to support the change. EBITDA is the primary measure of our ongoing business performance, and maximizing this through 2006 will be important as we need to maximize our profits during this period of tight supply of materials and high margins.

– *Significantly reduce total transformation cost structure to gain competitive advantage, maximize EBITDA, and enable future outsourcing.* We must begin aggressively gaining cost improvements from the Lean work being undertaken. The transformation costs of core products including production costs and material scrap during conversion from raw material to finished products must be driven lower to maintain our current competitive position now and into the future. It is also critical to be the cost and technical leader in core manufacturing in North America to enable future outsourcing projects and maintain existing large clients.

– *Achieve substantial/profitable sales growth in core products, and maintain strong steel slitting supply position.* We must further target and expand core outsourcing with the North American transformer industry, and be the manufacturer of choice of these products. As many of these projects require a long sales cycle, we must maintain an industry presence and reputation, as well as develop long-term strategic relationships with transformer manufacturers. Maintaining a strong position as an excellent processor and supplier of electrical steels builds on our "expert" position in the industry and will assist in the further expansion of relationships with the industry.

- *Increase our knowledge of the value we provide to customers, and be the best at fulfilling what customers need and value.* We do not have a clear enough understanding of the value that we provide to customers. We are looked at by many customers as a cost—not as a part of the value chain. We must change this perception to create opportunities for growth and sustainability. We must understand what they value, measure their feedback regularly, and aggressively become the best at providing that to them. We must be exceptional on the basics—OTIF, fast deliveries, low product failure rate, and highly responsive.

- *Establish exceptional relationships with our employees, ensuring that we have a clear focus on their job fulfillment, needs, and well-being.* This will enable us to attain greatest levels of productivity from our employees, and seek to achieve a high level of employee flexibility, motivation, and customer focus. Employee health and well-being are critical to advancing the Lean culture and continuous improvement in our organization. Our employees must be led by positive, proactive leaders—creating an interdependent organization philosophy and attitude. Our employees at all levels of the organization must be provided with strong leadership and direction, and we must differentiate ourselves as an employer that truly values the contributions of all employees.

– *Create a culture of innovation and creativity, with a strong track record of new products and services focused on the North American transformer market.* In the past we have relied on expanding existing products and leveraging our supply position for growth. We must become a leader in innovation and new products to sustain our growth and profitability for the future. The current state will not last forever; and when the current market supply shortage goes away, we will enter challenging times to maintain financial performance.

3. Sales team CSFs:
   – Accurate analysis of markets and competitors.
   – Understand customer values/satisfaction and exceed expectations.
   – Focus on new business—added value.
   – Proactive/skilled KAM.
   – Generate correct RFQs—in line with business objectives.
   – *Improve speed of quotation.*
   – Improve conversion rate.

In this example, the Sales Team identifies the speed of quotation as a target for improvement. First, the *current state* is mapped and measures and targets are defined (Table 3.1).

Before the *future state* is developed, they align these to the strategy. They assess how difficult or easy it would

Table 3.1 Sales process targets and measures.

Sales Measure	Today	End 04	End 05	End 06	Vision
Date of receipt to date of quote					
Simple inquiry—C	10	10	8	5	3
Medium complexity—B	15	15	14	1	10
Very complex—A	40	40	33	25	20
Number of new key accounts contacted per year—resulting in a qualified inquiry	?	?	10	15	12
Number of RFQs per qtr					
New tooling	?	?	7	10	11
Catalog types (minimum value)	?	?	10	15	17
Conversion rate of RFQs **First follow up on quotes sent out within no later than x days**	**5–50+**	**5–50+**	**10**	**5**	**3 working days**
Market share					
Existing customers					
Overall laminations market (Europe)	23%	23%			?
Self producers)					
Number of new initiatives with customers	Ad hoc	0	1	2	3
Customer satisfaction	32%	40%	50%	60%	67%

be to implement the potential improvements and what the impact would be on the business and the customer (Table 3.2). Reducing the time taken to process requests for quotation (RFQs) would have a major impact both on the business and on the customer, so this becomes part of the Lean management system, and teams are given the resources to improve the process.

Whether it is on the shop floor or in the support offices, well-designed processes should always be aligned with the strategy and part of the Lean management system. The same business cockpits used to manage shop-floor processes can also be used to manage commercial and support areas. Having the same Lean management system helps to engage everyone in the organization and demonstrates to the commercial areas that they are also part of the Lean journey.

Table 3.2 Impact and difficulty of improvement opportunities.

	Critical Success Factors	Impact	
		Business	Customer
1	Accurate analysis of markets and competitors	H	M
2	Understand customer values/satisfaction and exceed expectations	H	H
3	Focus on new business—added value	H	H
4	Proactive/skilled KAM	H	H
5	Generate correct RFQs—in line with business objectives	H	H
6	Improve speed of quotation	H	H
7	Improve conversion rate	H	M

I chose Lean to give the business direction and vision. One of the very appealing sides of the Lean is to give employees perspective and to get them to think about the problems and to involve them in all of the decisions. Whether people are on the shop floor, the sales office or the board room, it is about making them aware of the bigger picture and how they can influence it. It is my personal belief that the issue of motivation of people is all about giving them a chance to influence.

—Marcel, Managing Director

The secret of good planning and strategy is to tell convincing "stories" that people can relate to and understand. The Lean way of doing this is known as "A3 thinking." In this we develop strategies that can be described on one side of an A3 sheet of paper. The strategy (at any level) should read as a persuasive "story." It starts in the top left-hand corner (shown in Figure 3.7) by stating the strategic gap and then it reads up and down, from left to right. The strategic gap is followed by a reflection on the reasons why the gap has not been breached in the past; this is often shown as a fishbone diagram. This is followed by a Pareto analysis of the reasons for the gap and an action plan of countermeasures, targets, and contingencies.

D: Doing Phase

After the planning cycle (P) comes the doing phase (D). This is the start of deploying the policy; the idea here is to engage and involve everyone. The way that companies such as Cogent Power and Toyota do this is by a mechanism known as "Catchball." Catchball is described by Michael Cowley and Ellen Domb in *Beyond Strategic*

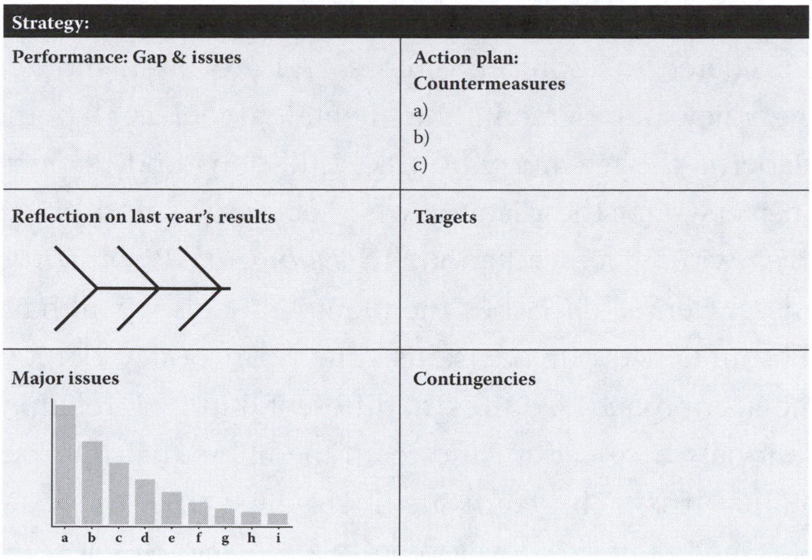

Figure 3.7   A3 strategic thinking.

Vision: Effective Corporate Action with Hoshin Planning as the thing that makes policy deployment different from Management by Objectives. In Catchball, the plans are shared horizontally and vertically throughout the organization, level by level, and questions such as "What do you think?" or "Why can't we achieve this?" are asked. This encourages frank, fact-based discussion and leverages the collective knowledge and intelligence of the organization to make the plans achievable.

The Catchball process gets people involved and encourages buy-in as employees are given the opportunity to participate in setting realistic targets and KPIs. The Catchball phase is important as it allows problems to be raised. In the Lean world, problems are considered treasures because, without problems and problem solving, an organization cannot improve. This involves a set of mental models that is different from those of traditional organizations where problems are considered to represent failure and are often hidden. In policy deployment, the mental model is that the leader is the teacher who asks questions and respects answers—not the dictator who sets targets and objectives without consultation. In *Doing the Right Thing*, Pascal Dennis describes the mental models we all have that influence our decisions. The Lean policy deployment approach requires a different kind of relationship between leaders and team members that involves mutual trust. The team members must trust the leaders' judgment in developing plans, and the leaders must trust the team members' knowledge and ability to deploy the plans. There is more about this in the next chapter; for now, we will stay with the PDCA of strategy and alignment.

C: Check Phase

The next steps are to perform the actions and review progress. This is the check phase (C), where the plan is monitored and problems raised. It seems simple but this is the phase that often fails in traditional planning. Check entails simple connected meetings where exceptions are shared and discussed openly; back to the Lean mental models of problems being treasured as opportunities for improvement. Policy deployment is a formal process and the key to it is the review process.

Cowley and Domb, in their book entitled *Beyond Strategic Vision: Effective Corporate Action with Hoshin Planning,* describe the process and suggest three levels of review (shown in Figure 3.8):

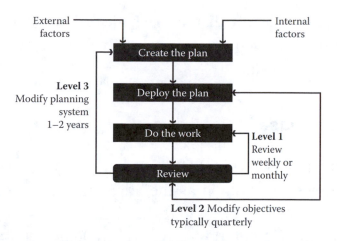

Figure 3.8 Strategic alignment and deployment process. (*Source:* Michael Cowley and Ellen Domb, *Beyond Strategic Vision: Effective Corporate Action with Hoshin Planning*, 1997.)

1. Review the work done on a weekly or monthly cycle.
2. Review the key issues on a monthly or quarterly cycle.
3. Review the planning system as a whole on an annual or biannual cycle to ensure that it works for your organization.

As the Lean implementation matures, the organization learns from the process, and new opportunities open up that were impossible when it first started. The skill is to take advantage of the new opportunities and to remain focused on steering in the right direction. Cogent Power has done this by maintaining alignment and using the business cockpits to monitor progress. As the organization has learned from the process, it has used the knowledge, skills, and improved process capacity to introduce new products and business offerings that have enhanced customer satisfaction. The organizational learning has been so successful that new markets have developed that were not even on the horizon when the Lean program was introduced.

A: Act Phase

The final phase of the PDCA cycle is the act phase (A), sometimes also known as the adjust phase. This is the problem-solving phase, and the focus here is to maintain alignment with the goals, so problems that emerge and disrupt the flow should be addressed. Problems are usually distributed (see Figure 3.9); there will be two or three large problems, ten or so mid-size problems, and generally hundreds of small problems. It is these small issues that cause irritation or frustration; if you can solve these, many of the larger problems disappear.

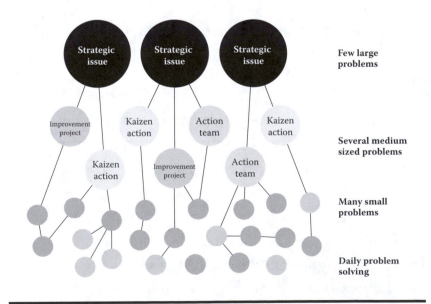

Figure 3.9 Cascade of problems and solutions. (*Source: Dennis Pascal, Strategy deployment: What is it and why should I care? Lean Enterprise Institute Webinar, 2007.*)

However, there are usually too many for a small group of people to solve, so problem solving should be shared and distributed throughout the organization.

This again involves different mental models. In the traditional organization, there are specialists, usually engineers, who use complex tools to solve problems. This "expert" problem solving is often done "to" people and, hence, disengages the workforce. The Lean organization recognizes that most problems can be solved without complex tools. So the mental model here is to involve everyone in problem solving, using simple tools, leaving the specialists to concentrate on the large, complex problems.

Summary

In summary, strategy and alignment are about setting the direction for the organization and making sure that everyone is on board so that the organization stays on course and maintains steady progress. Strategy and alignment are based on policy deployment, developed from Deming's scientific method and the PDCA cycle. It can be summarized as Figure 3.10.

Anything you might do based on the learning from this book from this point on will be like pouring water on sand if you do not adequately address your strategy and alignment. Indeed, this area is often the weakest spot for many organizations we see. As a warning, we will now list what we frequently see within this area:

- Little or no visual management at operational levels
- People not knowing what they are really trying to achieve

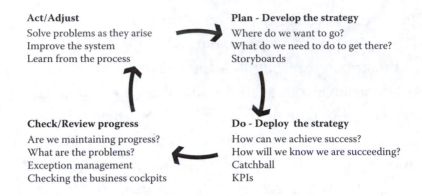

Act/Adjust
Solve problems as they arise
Improve the system
Learn from the process

Plan - Develop the strategy
Where do we want to go?
What do we need to do to get there?
Storyboards

Check/Review progress
Are we maintaining progress?
What are the problems?
Exception management
Checking the business cockpits

Do - Deploy the strategy
How can we achieve success?
How will we know we are succeeding?
Catchball
KPIs

Figure 3.10 Dr. Deming's scientific method and PDCA applied to strategy alignment and deployment.

- Frustrated Lean coaches "pushing" solutions on reluctant busy line staff
- Frustrated senior managers not understanding why people "don't get it"
- Most measures are backward looking
- Approximately 50 percent of KPIs get changed
- Frequent gaps in the strategy
- Lots of wasted opportunities as only a low percentage of people are aligned with strategy

If this sounds like you, we suggest that you reread this chapter before progressing.

Strategy and alignment learning points can be summarized as follows:

- Take time to define clear and stretching CSFs and build in a PDCA cycle to improve the deployment process.
- Work to build up the capability of individuals and teams to self-manage the business cockpits at all levels.

■ Deploy words and numbers to ensure that full "Line of Sight" is achieved; people know the business plans and their contribution in making it happen.

Use our template (see Figure 8.13a) in Chapter 8 to assess how well strategy and alignment are deployed in your organization.

Chapter 4

Leadership

Leadership is often seen as the holy grail of successful management. Indeed, poor leadership has been identified as the reason for poor sustainability of Lean change, as the top ten reasons for failure in Table 4.1 reveal. These findings (Table 4.1) are based on a review of the major issues leading to poor sustainability across a range of manufacturing and distribution organizations.

We have found that there is often some confusion between management and leadership. Many people talk about managing transformations rather than leading change. This may sound like a subtle difference, but it

Table 4.1 Top ten reasons for failure.

1. Lack of a clear executive vision.
2. Lack of an effective communication strategy.
3. Failure to create and communicate a real sense of urgency.
4. Poor consultation with stakeholders.
5. Lack of structured methodology and project management.
6. Failure to monitor and evaluate the outcome.
7. Failure to mobilize change champions.
8. Failure to engage employees.
9. Absence of a dedicated and fully resourced implementation team.
10. Lack of sympathetic and supportive Human Resources policies.

is an important one. Warren Bennis, in *On Becoming a Leader* (2003), describes some of the differences he sees between managers and leaders (Table 4.2).

Think of some managers in your organization. Are they leaders or managers? Leaders, in our view, foster change and create an environment where change is the norm, whereas managers stabilize the organization and ensure that the changes are well implemented. In fact, both sets of behavior are necessary to achieve excellence, and different approaches may be needed at different times, depending on where you are in the transformation. Also, leadership is not confined to the top level of an organization; leaders can emerge at all levels, and part of the role of managers is to recognize and develop potential leaders so that they can contribute to the business goals. Think about some of the other people in your organization—trade union shop stewards, supervisors, influential employees—how would you describe them?

Table 4.2   Differences between leaders and managers.

Leader	Manager
Innovates	Administers
Is an original	Is a copy
Develops	Maintains
Focuses on people	Focuses on systems and structure
Inspires trust	
Has a long-range perspective	Relies on control
Asks why	Has a short-range view
Has his eye on the horizon	Asks how and when
Originates	Has his eye on the bottom line
Challenges the status quo	Imitates
	Accepts the status quo

Source: Bennis, *On Becoming a Leader.*

Leadership is about establishing direction, developing a vision of the future, and setting strategies for making changes to achieve that vision. Leadership involves aligning people, communicating the direction by words and deeds to the entire workforce to get the cooperation that is needed. It is about influencing the creation of teams that understand the vision and accept their roles in the implementation of the strategy. It is really about inspiring people to want to change.

> My role has been to give the direction and perspective, to provide the means and resources, to support the people and protect them from criticism, but they have trained themselves in what was expected and they have executed Lean. I am quite happy with the way we implemented it. You can always say it could have been better, but I think we did very well. Anyway, sometimes you need failures to convince people what could have been done.
> —Marcel, Managing Director, Cogent Power Group

Level 5 Leadership

In *Good to Great* (1991), Jim Collins found that success is due primarily to the abilities, competence, and style of the leader. He identifies five levels of leadership (Figure 4.1), with the highest level leading to the most sustainable and effective business.

> Level 5 leaders channel their ego away from themselves and into the larger goal of building a great company. It's not that Level 5 leaders have no ego or self-interest. Indeed, they are incredibly ambitious—but their ambition is first and foremost for the institution, not themselves. (p. 21)

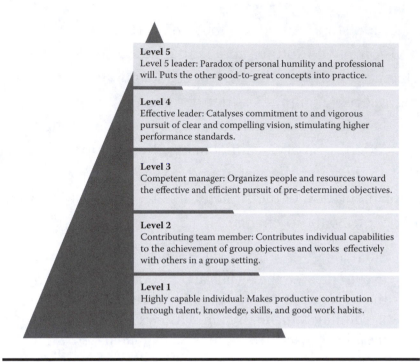

Figure 4.1 **Level 5 leadership. (*Source:* Jim Collins, *From Good to Great*, 2001.)**

Terry Leahy (Tesco's chief executive) and Fujio Cho (the chairman of Toyota) are good examples of Level 5 leaders.

In a radio broadcast, Peter Day (Presenter, BBC Radio 4 and BBC World Service, June 26, 2007) described Fujio Cho, chairman of Toyota, as shy: "Mr. Cho has only been in the top job at Toyota for a year, and he is only the second chairman not to be a member of the founding family.

"But he's been with the Japanese automotive giant since 1960. He is now 70, not particularly old by the standards of Japanese bosses. Mr. Cho got a law degree from the elite Tokyo University, and then joined Toyota as an apprentice.

"He learnt the secrets of Toyota's revolutionary Lean Manufacturing System from the man who invented it, Taiichi Ohno, an unarguable genius.

In the six years from 1988, Mr. Cho was the head of Toyota's United States operation in Kentucky at a time of relentless and brave expansion, a long way from home. He must have picked up a lot of English, but he prefers to speak Japanese when answering reporters' questions. I suppose it gives him time to think, and thinking is what he does, leaving quite long gaps between a question and its tentative answer. Mr. Cho does not wish to appear to have all the answers. His is extraordinary modesty, and so is his company, considering what they have just done."

> It is a mistake to suppose that men succeed through success; they much oftener succeed through failures. Precept, study, advice, and example could never have taught them so well as failure has done.
> —Samuel Smiles, British author of *Self Help,* 1856 (favorite of Sakiichi Toyoda)

We observed a similar lack of ego in Marcel, Cogent Power's Managing Director. However, leadership is not just about the characteristics of the leaders. Jim Collins suggests that acquiring, or, more accurately, growing a Level 5 leader is just the first step. Once the right leader is in place, he or she must get the right team about them: "They *first* got the right people on the bus, the wrong people off the bus, and the right people in the right seats."

Over the past fifty years, much has been written and there have been numerous theories as to what constitutes leadership, and most have been a reflection on the circumstances of that particular time. It is true to say that leadership theories have evolved over time, with each new theory building on the previous one to explain the revelations as new leaders develop and emerge. We will explain a few of the more influential theories here that we saw demonstrated at Cogent Power, but this is not meant as a definitive guide.

Situational Leadership

"Situational" leadership is all about the right style of leadership at the right time. We might define four generic styles of leadership:

1. Telling
2. Selling
3. Participating
4. Delegating

All of these might have their place in different circumstances. For instance, when a new employee needs briefing about his new role, a *telling* style might be most appropriate. A *selling* style may be effectively used at the start of a new organizational change when it is necessary to engage people in wanting to change. In many instances, as described above, a *participating* leadership style might be required so that employees can feel part of the change—for instance, by taking part in setting their own KPIs. Finally, a *delegating* leadership style is appropriate when employees have high levels of skills and motivation and just need the opportunity to show what they can do.

It is our experience that the style most leaders find most difficult to achieve is the delegating style. Ask yourself the following questions. Do you find that you take on far too many things? Are there activities that might be better done by your team? Do you find it difficult to let go? Would you benefit by having less to deal with so you can concentrate on your vital few?

Distributed or Dispersed Leadership

Distributed or dispersed leadership appears to present something a little different and, in a generic sense, represents the decentralization of leadership skills and responsibilities in an organization.

The distinctive characteristic of distributed leadership is that it is seen as emerging from a collective, or conjoint, activity and is seen as an emergent property of a group or team.

Simply put, distributed leadership refers to spreading the responsibilities of leadership across the organization where leaders can be developed at every level, rather than having just one leader at the top of an organization. In a journal article, Gary Yukl (1999) explains that distributed leadership "does not require an individual who can perform all of the essential leadership functions, only a set of people who can collectively perform them."

The development of distributed leadership theories has been in response to the criticism that some forms of leadership have difficulty accommodating changes in the division of labor in the workplace, particularly new patterns of interdependence and coordination.

The first framework of a developing dispersed leadership writing was outlined in 1993 by Katzenbach and Smith, in which they presented the value of *real teams*:

teams "with a small number of people with complementary skills who are committed to a common performance purpose, performance goals, and approach for which they hold themselves mutually accountable." The concept of self-leadership, which is inherent in dispersed leadership, enables leaders to facilitate individuals to develop their leadership skills and "turn their constituents into leaders," building on the idea that a leader empowers his (her) followers by teaching them to lead themselves—a theme that is present in the work of Burns and his theory on transforming leadership.

Studies detailing the impact of leadership practices in today's economic climate highlight the demands for an alternative way of thinking in order to sustain a high-performance environment. It is necessary that leadership practices transcend organizational and individual constraints and successfully deal with change—practices that are necessary in today's knowledge economy. Distributed leadership practices are necessary in allowing leaders to develop team-based and networked relationships and can be better understood as fluid and emergent, rather than a fixed structure.

We have found that, in a successful and sustainable Lean transformation, the style of leadership and the role and responsibilities of leaders change during the initiation and implementation to reflect the changing role of the leaders. A clear vision and clarity of communicating the need for change is important in the decision-making initiation phase, and it is the role of senior management to "sell" the vision to the employees and convince them of the need to change. The style of leadership here is to inspire and encourage employees to follow. The message must be simple and unambiguous so that it can be clearly understood. The leaders must be able to overcome organizational (not invented here) and political resistance, where managers fear a loss of status, power, and control described by Eckes in his book entitled *Making Six Sigma Last*.

Kurt Lewin, the psychologist, describes this as the "unfreeze" phase of change. John Lucey (2008) mapped the reasons for failure of Lean transformations onto the Lewin Unfreeze, Change, and Refreeze model. We have adapted this in Table 4.3 to show the relative importance of each reason.

The unfreeze phase calls for a leader with clarity and vision to set direction while change and refreeze phases call for dispersed, adaptive leadership that can manage the change process with appropriate HR policies, to recruit, train, reward, and recognize and this is seen by team leaders and managers who "walk the talk" and whose presence on the shop floor is highly visible, as demonstrated in Gemba management.

A bottom-up Lean transformation that starts with low-cost/no-cost improvements may start with adaptive change and dispersed leadership, shown in Figure 4.2. However, if this is to proceed to adopting Lean thinking across the whole organization, it will be necessary to move to transformational change to align the change process with strategy to prevent fragmentation of the implementation and policies. The transition from "push" to "pull" is usually a fairly large jump that is difficult to break down into incremental steps of implementation and must be taken in one stride. This requires strong senior management commitment to support the change.

Table 4.3   Reasons for failure mapped to stages of change.

Phase	Reason For Failure	Importance
Unfreeze (Plan and Prepare Phase)	Lack of clear executive vision and leadership	9
	Lack of effective communication strategy	9
	Failure to create a sense of urgency	8
	Poor consultation with all stakeholders	7
	Failure to recognize company history and culture	2
	Unrealistic plans	2
	Lack of project planning	7
Change (Implementation Phase)	Failure to mobilize change champions	6
	Lack of dedicated implementation team	4
	Lack of appropriate HR policies	4
	Poor management of quick wins	1
	Relying on external consultant	1
Refreeze (Embed Change)	Failure to monitor and evaluate	6
	Failure to engage employees	5
	Failure to celebrate & recognize success	1

Source: Adapted from John Lucey. (2008), unpublished PHD Thesis, Cardiff University.

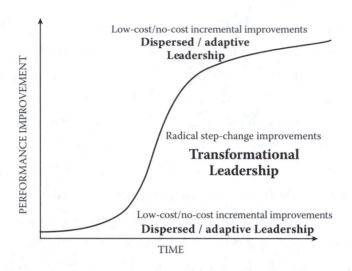

Figure 4.2 How leadership styles might change during Lean transformations.

Once the policies and strategy have been set, the implementation can then move once more into an adaptive mode to pursue continuous improvement where change is incremental.

The role of the senior managers is to set the key performance indicators (KPIs) that are aligned to the strategy. The role of the dispersed leaders is to cascade, measure, and monitor them, and to encourage and coach the problem solving and problem resolutions that maintain them. It has been shown that rewards are important where leaders impose change and do not involve people, but are less important when people are clear about the reason and have an opportunity to become involved. This suggests that a coaching style is important during the implementation phase of change, and that rewards are less significant when leaders adopt this style.

Both leaders and managers are important in a Lean transformation. Strategic (or transformational) leadership is about making decisions, creating vision, and allocating resources. Supervisory (or transactional) leadership, or management, is intended to provide support, guidance, and feedback on a day-to-day basis. Supervisory (or transactional) leadership is about motivating followers by clarifying their role, meeting their social needs, and providing them with appropriate rewards. This form of leadership is often very efficient, but because it essentially relies on maintaining the status quo and following established rules, it does not provide an organization with the scope for significant change. When radical change is required, transformational leadership is often necessary. Transformational leaders are able to bring about radical change, or turnaround, within an organization. Rather than utilizing rewards and incentives, transformational leaders rely on more abstract qualities such as using vision and values to convince their staff to work in the best interests of the collective organization. The vision presented by the leader is so appealing that followers are prepared to make sacrifices and work harder in order to achieve it, often changing the organizational culture in the process.

There is more evidence of transformational leadership at senior management levels than at other levels, probably because senior managers have more opportunity to change organizations through strategic decision making. This supports our view that senior managers are responsible for initiating Lean change and setting the strategic vision while the implementation and sustainability of the change involves day-to-day support and coaching by managers who "walk the talk." This implies that, in more mature Lean transformations, the leadership is devolved and dispersed throughout the organization in a network of group, and team, leaders who take the responsibility for adaptive change and continuous improvement.

When Marcel joined Cogent Power in 2003, he already had the experience of working in a Lean organization. His background was in automotive, so he needed no convincing of the benefits of implementing Lean thinking in a company. He was absolutely positive that this was the right path for Cogent Power to follow; all he needed to do, in the spirit of transformational leadership, was to gain the same level of conviction from the employees. This was not too difficult as the company had a history of continual improvement and total quality management (TQM) with a project called Transformational Mapping (TMAP), which was based on a number of Lean principles. Although the earlier initiatives had not sustained beyond the implementation phase, they did provide a foundation of change management, and a number of the Lean coaches and change agents came from running TMAP projects. Marcel's vision was that Cogent Power would become a self-propelling organization, an organization able to move forward by its own force. Ron, the Divisional Director, at Cogent Power Canada, developed a cartoon (Figure 4.3) that symbolized a self-propelling organization to communicate the idea to the workforce.

Marcel arrived in August 2003 but stayed in the background for the first few months. During this time, he was developing the strategy and assessing the organization, making sure that it was capable of fulfilling his vision. During this time, he held intensive interviews with all the managers and key people, in which he asked very searching and challenging questions. He described this time in terms of his favorite hobby, training horses:

The Vision

Figure 4.3   Cogent Power's vision: A self-propelling organization.

> There is only one way to train a horse, and that's from a positive attitude. You have got to have an eye for positive development and make the horse aware of the fact that you like what he is doing and, whenever he does something negative, you ignore it. Of course, first of all, you've got to be sure that the material, the horse itself, is capable of doing the things you want him to do. If it has only three legs, you probably wouldn't want to train it. It is the same with an organization; you have to be sure that the people you've got on board can deliver. If you are not sure at the start of the program and you find out later that they can't, it won't make sense to punish them. That is basically where I come from.

His commitment involved some hard decisions and a reorganization of the management team. To assist him, he invited Frans, a former colleague, to join him as Technology Director. They made a formidable team, highly respected and hugely influential.

> Marcel raised the bar and set the standards, he was the person telling us what was expected of us; Frans was the person showing us the way.
> —Mark, General Manager, Cogent Power, United Kingdom

Jim Collins found that focus and perseverance were necessary: "You must maintain unwavering faith that you can and will prevail in the end, regardless of the difficulties, *AND at the same time* have the discipline to confront brutal facts of your current reality, whatever they might be," (*Good to Great*, HarperCollins, New York, 1991, p. 86). This was also true at Cogent Power, but added to this was Marcel's emphasis on trust—not only on being trustworthy himself, but also on trusting his management team to deliver the results, and on trusting that the organization was actually capable of change.

> Trustworthiness is paramount to make a success of whatever you do in life. When we asked him how he communicated the need for change, he answered, "It was only me, telling the truth."
> —Marcel, Managing Director, Cogent Power Group

Trust pervades the company and this is very important to sustaining change, as Ron told us:

> One of the things that helped the implementation was the trust relationship. Because of this, they accepted that I knew what I was talking about and that I had their best interests at heart. I'm not naïve enough to think that everybody thought that way, but there is a general trust. When I started in this company, it was not in a good way and one of the first things I did was to raise wages and this got cooperation and as a result the business grew, so they believed in me.

So how do leaders manage Lean organizations? In a recent presentation, Jim Womack said that every organization must address the *purpose,* the *processes,* and the *people*. He believes that most organizations struggle because the purpose is not clearly defined, the processes are not clearly specified, and the people are not fully engaged. In his view, getting this right is the responsibility of the leaders and management. Womack believes that one of the problems is that traditional organizations have a vertical focus, and managers think vertically to optimize their area, department, or function. Lean managers, on the other hand, think horizontally, in the direction that value flows through the organization. This is not to say that functions are less strong in Lean organizations. In many cases, including Toyota, they are even stronger. Lean organizations create strong horizontal focus by assigning a responsible person to manage product flow at the same time as they create strong functions that focus on knowledge capture and career paths. Toyota does this via the chief engineer role. The chief engineer at Toyota takes responsibility for the whole value chain of a particular product, from design to delivery. However, this is not a matrix organization where people have two bosses; the chief engineer must negotiate with the functional heads about what is needed from the functions to support the product. Every employee has only one boss: the functional head, who has to prioritize the work schedules.

At Cogent Power, Lean Managers fulfill this horizontal, cross-functional role and negotiate with functional heads to train employees and to give them time to work on improvement projects. Lean coaches, who form part of the functional teams, provide resources that support process improvements within the department and participate in cross-functional teams that perform company-wide improvements.

In Lean organizations, functions are the home base for employees: the place where deep technical or specialist knowledge is created and where career paths are guided. However, they succeed because they think in process terms.

Marcel and Frans do not believe that managing Lean is the job of one individual or one department. They believe that it is the responsibility of all managers, and that the responsibility starts with spending time with front-line workers: going to the *Gemba*, or place where the action is happening. *Gemba management* is a critical element of Lean leadership, crucial to sustaining Lean. Leaders must be seen to be "walking the talk" and leading by example. To do this, they must spend time on the shop floor, or in the data processing offices, where they can observe first-hand what is going on.

> Management, or leadership, is not sitting in an office. Management is being on the floor, including HR, at least 2 hours each day.
> —Frans, Technology Director, Cogent Power Group

When Ron first took over at Cogent Power's Canadian plant, he spent most of his time on the shop floor. By doing this, he established strong relationships with the workforce and built up trust in his leadership.

> I have been in this business for 11 years and, for the first 5 or 6 years, I spent more than 50 percent of my time on the shop floor every day. This is where I built the reputation and the trust. Employees feel free to contact me directly, which extends beyond the core of the 80 or 90 production workers who

> have been here all this time, and who I have developed the sort of relationship with. They feel that I can relate to them individually. I have also had new guys, who I have barely met, who have come to me for advice. I grew up on a dairy farm. So I had humble beginnings, and I think this has helped my attitude and approach.
>
> —Ron, Divisional Director, Cogent Power, Canada

John Shook was the first American manager at Toyota Japan, and he thinks that the leader's job at Toyota is, first, to get everyone to take the initiative to solve problems and, second, to ensure that everyone's job is aligned with the company's goals. It is the leader's job to develop people by mentoring, coaching, and example.

The following text is taken from Cogent Power's *Lean Management System Handbook* and shows that Gemba management and managing by fact is central to Cogent Power's Lean lifestyle.

> Gemba is the Japanese term for 'actual place,' and describes the place where value-creating work for a customer occurs. Real improvement or problem solving can only take place when there is a front-line focus and a very clear understanding of the process—from the point of view of those operating. Specifically, the term 'Go to the Gemba' refers to the expectation that leaders and support teams need to go the place the actual work is being undertaken to effectively solve a problem or understand the facts of a specific situation or circumstance. Do not assume or theorize, go to where the work is being performed, observe with your own eyes and ask questions to understand. This often refers to shop floor work and processes; however the same can be said

for work on any process. You must get out of your office or work space to where the work is being done. 'Managing by fact' is an important part of Lean thinking. Not knowing the correct facts or data will lead to incorrect information, lead to very poor problem solving, and will be a source of waste. Avoid making careless assumptions, as this will lead to creating more waste and less customer value.

—*Thinking Lean: Cogent Lean Management Handbook,* Ron and Greg, Cogent Power, Canada.

We previously discussed mental models that influence our decision making. In *The Fifth Discipline*, Senge describes mental models as one of the five learning disciplines that build learning capabilities in an organization. Mental models are the discipline of reflection and enquiry focused around developing awareness and attitudes that influence thoughts and decisions. The Toyota leadership model is a good example (Figure 4.4) of this

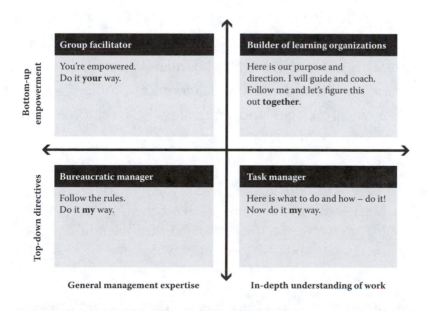

Figure 4.4　Toyota leadership model.

as it relies on very different mental models than those found in many traditional organizations. Leaders or managers of traditional organizations tend to follow either the old "dictator style," often referred to as *command and control*, or the laissez-faire "empowerment style" of the 1980s.

A generalist manager with a command-and-control mental model delivers top-down directives and expects people to "follow the rules." His or her approach might be to "Do it my way," while a top-down task manager might say, "This is what to do and how to do it—now do it my way."

Managers or leaders holding a bottom-up "empowerment" mental model might take a different approach and say, "You are empowered to make the decisions. This is what I want to achieve; I don't care how you go about it, as long as you deliver the results—do it your way." In contrast, Toyota leaders want to know enough technical details to understand the problem and appreciate the solution but their approach would be to "Follow me and let us figure this out together." The Lean leader style is that of a mentor, coach, and active participant in problem solving. This is what engages and motivates the workforce.

> To be a truly effective and sustainable Lean enterprise, we believe that the leader's role is to set the direction and inspire people to achieve this—in other words, the WHAT and WHY. However, their role is to trust the employee to come up with the plan—in other words, the HOW.

Lean leaders also understand that a good financial performance is a result of a well-managed process, and that financial results reflect the control and performance of the process. As Frans told us:

> If you are doing the right things then the bottom line results will follow; if you constantly chase the bottom line then this may result in doing the wrong things.

This has certainly been true for Cogent Power as, by doing the right things, they have turned the company around from loss-making to highly profitable within three years. Mark, the general manager at the UK factory, believes strongly that success comes not only from doing things right, but also from doing the right things. He uses the efficiency/effectiveness matrix (Figure 4.5) to put Lean into context and to illustrate to his team the need for being both efficient and effective.

Leadership is important at every stage of Lean transformation, but particularly at the start and during the "it isn't worth it" phase when management typically

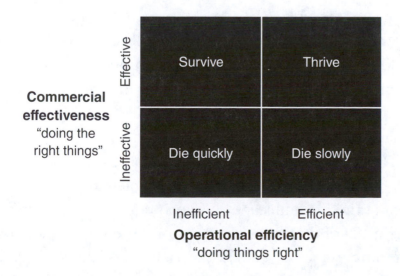

Figure 4.5 Operational efficiency vs. commercial effectiveness.

becomes extremely unhappy as the benefits often appear smaller than the pain of gaining them, usually somewhere between 18 and 24 months after starting a transformation. It was during this period that Cogent Power recognized that the middle managers were struggling. Early emphasis had been on developing the senior management team, who were responsible for driving the change, and the Lean coaches, who were going to train shop-floor operators in Lean improvements and problem solving. This top-down and bottom-up approach had neglected the middle managers, who were being asked to manage the Lean transition but did not have the same level of skills as the people they were managing.

> What we left out in the beginning was the middle management. We corrected this later, but we missed it in the beginning, and it caused us some problems.
> —Frans, Technology Director, Cogent Power Group

To reengage the middle managers, Peter, the HR Director, developed a Lean management training program for all the managers across all sites (Figure 4.6). The program was based on the fourteen Toyota Way Principles described by Jeffrey Liker in *The Toyota Way* and by Douglas Howardell in *Seven Lean Skills* (see next chapter).

The program, with the aim of helping individuals and teams to "lead the Lean lifestyle," integrated the latest Lean thinking and leadership techniques with the strategic goals of the business. Much of the emphasis was on the importance of values and behaviors that would be needed to lead the organization into the next phase of maturity. All attendees had to commit formally to leading

Senior level leadership
Making informed strategic choices on the continuous improvement systems and behaviors that best align to the future needs of the business.

Middle level leadership
Aligning future roles of operational leaders and their teams to meet the business goals and deploying a process for continuous and sustainable improvement.

Local level leadership
Understanding the needs of the local area, in order to lead and enable the team to sustain continuous improvement.

Figure 4.6   Multi-level leadership program.

a Lean improvement activity in their area in order to support the business; the program provided a fresh impetus to the Lean journey just at the right time. The result was that line managers and team leaders were given skills that emphasized the change in roles and responsibilities expected of the entire leadership community as it went forward.

The program challenged individuals continuously to push themselves and their teams out of the "comfort zone" and into the "stretch zone." Managers were taught not simply to look at reducing *muda*, but also to take responsibility for reducing *mura* and *muri* (Figure 4.7).

It is the leader's responsibility to develop people. This means constantly moving them out of their comfort zone and stretching them a little, but there is a balance here that can be explained in terms of *muda, mura,* and *muri*.

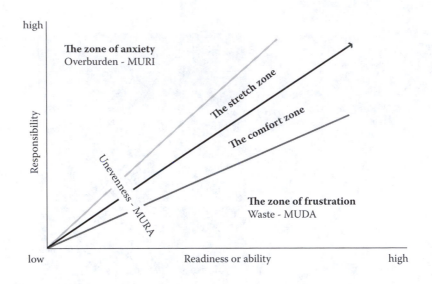

Figure 4.7   The STRETCH zone. (*Source:* Adapted from Mihaly Csikszentmihalyi, *Flow: The Psychology of Optimal Experience.* New York: Harper and Row 1990.)

During one of the leadership sessions, Cosimo (a production manager at the Canadian plant) explained how, when he first was asked to manage a new *pull* system (see Chapter 7 on Technology, Tools, and Techniques), that he was "off the scale" in the zone of anxiety as he was nowhere near ready for the responsibility that had been handed to him. Within six months of working on the pull system, Cosimo reflected on his position and announced that he was now in "the comfort zone" and needed another challenge.

Continuous improvement aims to develop people so that they stay just above the comfort zone. Lean is about more than continuous improvement; it is also about *respect for people*. This means avoiding the zone of anxiety where employees feel overstretched and are given responsibility beyond their readiness or ability.

Respect for people also means keeping them out of the zone of frustration by respecting their abilities and pushing them gently to achieve more. At Cogent Power the employees constantly strive to keep in the stretch zone, and the managers and leaders know and appreciate the dangers of human resource *muda, mura,* and *muri*.

> The "Respect for People" aspect of lean thinking often gets heavily overshadowed by the continuous improvement aspect of lean. 'Respect for People' is equal to or greater than the continuous improvement element in realizing the potential of a lean enterprise, since without respect for people sustainable improvement is impossible. Respect for people has two simple aspects.
>
> **RESPECT**—We respect others, make every effort to understand each other, take responsibility and do our best to build mutual trust.
>
> **TEAMWORK**—We stimulate personal and professional growth, share the opportunities of development and maximize individual and team performance. The 'Respect for People' principle encompasses all key stakeholders: employees, suppliers, customers, investors, and communities. The 'Respect for People' principle is founded on the belief that team members are allowed and expected to realize their potential through active participation in running and improving their work and work processes; and are given a high level of ownership and accountability for creating and implementing work improvements in the processes they work in and achieving the desired results.
>
> —*Thinking Lean: Cogent Power Lean Management System Handbook,* Ron and Greg, Cogent Power, Canada.

In *The Exceptional Manager: Making the Difference,* Delbridge, Gratton, and Johnson provide insight into the qualities of exceptional managers and how they can make a difference. Exceptional managers are able to step out of their comfort zones and display the qualities of commitment and trust that they expect of others. They champion a learning environment, are participative, and have the capacity to challenge and reflect. Exceptional managers engage others in reflective conversations that help the company on its journey to sustainable long-term prosperity. These are some of the qualities that are observed in the managers and leaders at Cogent Power; they are observed in abundance in Marcel and Frans.

Summary

Leadership is a key part of the "below the waterline" part of the Lean Iceberg. To be successful, we all need to do more than just manage today; we need to inspire tomorrow. To do this requires self-awareness and a willingness to adapt different management and leadership styles both during a workday, but more importantly as Lean matures in our organization.

There are, of course, a number of pitfalls in this area. Here are some of the things that we frequently encounter:

- Organizations have trained people to manage but rarely to lead.
- Most people only exhibit one leadership style: push.
- We fail to inspire our people.
- We do not listen to the voice of the employees.
- "Managers know best" thinking.
- A lot of wasted opportunities as few are inspired to change, certainly not in a sustainable way.

If this sounds like you, we suggest you do some more serious research and thinking on this topic. The leadership learning points can by summarized as follows:

- Strong decisive leadership with Lean experience is needed in the early phases of the program.
- The later phases require more dispersed or adaptive leadership that takes more hands-on responsibility and leads the incremental continuous improvement.
- Leaders must be prepared to review themselves critically, and the process, in order to push the business forward.
- Continually develop Lean leaders at all levels, on all shifts, and within all areas of the business and adopt a "leading the Lean lifestyle" program.

Use our template (at the back of the book) to assess how good the leadership is in your organization.

Chapter 5

Behavior and Engagement

Companies initiating Lean change often focus on tools and techniques such as value stream mapping and 5S. Although this approach frequently leads to quick wins and helps foster confidence among employees, sustaining these improvements over the long term can be problematic.

Three important groups are often ignored:

1. Customers: The supposed focus of the first Lean principle.
2. The company itself: What are we doing that will benefit the company?
3. The employees: When we make any change, we always need to ask ourselves, "What's in it for the employees?"

This chapter concentrates on people and looks at how employees, at all levels of the organization, can be motivated to adopt Lean behaviors and become engaged in the transformation.

Why focus on the employees? For many people, organizataional change is associated with feelings of insecurity, uncertainly, and anxiety, often leading to lack of buy-in and employee resistance. Getting all employees on board from the outset is crucial to sustaining Lean change.

Michael Hammer, reflecting on the failures of business process reengineering (BPR), told the *Wall Street Journal* (November 26, 1996) that he, and other reengineering leaders, *forgot about people*. "I wasn't smart enough," he says. "I was reflecting my engineering background and was insufficiently appreciative of the human dimension. I've learned that's critical."

Marcel had a vision of Cogent Power as a self-propelling organization. He recognized that to achieve this required a change in culture, encouraging the right attitudes and developing capabilities. His leadership helped inspire a set of appropriate behaviors and high levels of engagement. In the Canadian plant, Ron took Marcel's vision

---

Self-propelling organizations:

We have talked at different times about the desire within a Lean-thinking company to be what is called a "self-propelling" organization. In the spirit of waste elimination and continuous improvement, this means that the organization as a whole has the attitude, the culture, and the capabilities at all levels within the organization to achieve continuous improvement and sustain itself in the future. It is an organization that does not require a management initiative, a customer initiative, a shareholder initiative to improve—it comes from the desire and the will of the people inside the organization.

This requires a commitment everywhere in the organization to improve and to eliminate those obstacles that delay, prevent, or inhibit improvements. It is management and leaders' responsibilities to ensure that the organization takes actions on all employees' ideas and suggestions for improvement, and that good ideas for improvement are acted on quickly so that wastes can be eliminated and improvements generated. It takes a whole cultural change to make this happen. This is our desire and our goal. We will continue to work at this until we achieve it.

and translated this into their flagship Lean identifier of a self-propelled organization across the plant.

In this chapter of our journey through the iceberg, we look at the types of behavior and attitudes we want to encourage and how people can be motivated to adopt them. We then discuss the importance of engagement and how to get people engaged with the organization and the Lean implementation process. But before we start, it is worth thinking about the organizational model and the skills and competencies of the people who will help drive the change.

Changing the Organization

Sometimes, changing the organization and getting the organizational model right involves making hard decisions. If some people are really not willing or able to make the change, it is better to take the decision to move them earlier rather than later when problems have arisen.

Within any organization there will be some people who will resist change and try to maintain the status quo, while others adapt quickly and easily. In *Who Moved My Cheese?*, Spencer Johnson tells a light-hearted story about four fictional characters (Sniff, Scurry, Hem, and Haw) who represent the different approaches people take to change. People like Sniff seek change and enjoy working in places that are constantly changing. Others, like Scurry, immediately jump into action to get things done when change happens. These people enjoy the activities and actions that facilitate change. Then there are the people who hem and haw. These people do not like change; they are comfortable with their old regime and will try to preserve it; they view change as a loss of something: power, status, responsibilities, privileges, etc. At first they will deny that there is a need for change and will feel resentful. The difference between these last two groups is that the Haws are open-minded. They eventually recognize that change is inevitable and that all that is holding them back is their own fear. Once this happens, they will start to change—first by accepting and then by enjoying, and finally they embrace the change and thrive in it. In contrast, the Hems never accept the need for change and feel they are victims. They think that change is risky and feel safer with what they know. This sense of false security gives them comfort; but when they realize that the real danger lies in not changing, then some of them will become Haws. In general, about 80 percent of the Hems will eventually change, or become ineffective, but some hardcore resistors, irrespective of all efforts, will always resist change. The Hems who remain become anchors and try to prevent change from happening; they may even try to sabotage it. This puts the organization in danger of stagnation. As much as organizations want to keep all their employees, sometimes, as a last resort, they have to let some people go.

At Cogent Power, people were given every chance to join in with Lean. They were given training and support but, inevitably, a few remained who were not prepared to change. These employees had to go, as they would not even be able to survive the change. In making the decision to replace them, a strong message was sent to all employees, a message that signaled that the leaders were very serious about Lean.

> We changed our management structure as we looked at our organization in terms of what we are trying to do with improvements in Lean. There were some key changes that we needed to make. Two out of four front-line supervisors were changed, and we lost two plant managers and three operators. We haven't hesitated to make the changes, which has been a big part of our success. We made it quite clear that the first plant manager was changed because he didn't agree with the initiatives and waste elimination, etc. So the statements were loud and clear. We had a guy in purchasing, basically an internal supplier, but he had a much bigger role in creating obstacles, so we let him go at the end of last year. But all of this takes time. We train them, we support them, we give them every opportunity to join in and to change, but at the end, sometimes you have to let them go. We had to make management, staff, and operational changes to succeed. If as an organization you are determined to make the change successful, you cannot be hesitant in removing key people if they are blocking progress; this is the message that I'm sending and I was quite conscious to make this message clear. You understand that if you have a vision of where you want to get to, you have to make changes in attitude and culture to get there, and you have to be tough enough to remove the obstacles in the way.
> —Ron, Transformer Divisional Director, Cogent Power, Canada

Before we consider Lean behaviors and behavioral change, let us think carefully for a moment why some people resist change.

> Before you start with Lean, you must be sure that you have the right organizational model and that these are the right people to make it work. If they're not the right people, it doesn't mean that Lean is not correct; it is the people that are wrong. I make the comparison with horses. If you have show jumpers and workhorses, you can train the workhorses all the time, but you will never make them jump. And it's the same with Lean; you need the right people to make sure it is a success.
> —Frans, Technology Director, Cogent Power Group

Overcoming Resistance to Change

Many people resist change through fear and this drives negative and defensive behaviors. Understanding resistance and working to remove it is critical to successful cultural and behavioral change. There are four basic forms of resistance: organizational, political, individualized, and technical (Table 5.1).

Think about the resistance you have encountered in your organization, or in yourself, and reflect on how it was expressed.

The most common form of resistance is technical resistance. This is where employees fear that they will not have the right skills to do the job and lack confidence. The right training and communication can help overcome this. We discuss training and communication more in the section on engagement.

Table 5.1 Forms of resistance.

Understanding Resistance	
Organizational resistance	Underlying issue is lack of control. Expressed as NIH (Not Invented Here)
Political resistance	When change is seen as a loss and/or threat to the status quo
Individualized resistance	Expressed as WIIIFM (What is in it for me?)
Technical resistance	Underlying issues are insecurity and concern that they understand how. What is not understood is often resisted. Expressed as being overwhelmed by the details

Source: Adapted from Eckes, 2001.

Political and organizational resistance is associated with perceived or real loss of control. In political resistance, this is a loss of power or position. Political resistance can be felt by anyone but it is most often associated with management resistance. Organizational resistance has more to do with loss of pride or ownership and is expressed as *Not Invented Here* (NIH) syndrome.

Sometimes, in any change, the loss is real and then support mechanisms are required to deal with the consequences of political and organizational resistance. Where the loss is perceived, making sure that people are given the opportunity to get involved, and are supported and encouraged in their new roles, should help alleviate it. But do not assume that this is easy. A lot of politics had to be dealt with at Cogent Power before Lean could be successfully deployed. It takes hard work and lots of effort to overcome political and organizational resistance.

Political resistors will try to maintain the status quo. In *Real Lean – Understanding the Lean Management System*, Emiliani explains that Real Lean means continuous improvement and respect for people. Fake Lean is where a company concentrates only on the continuous improvement and just deploys some Lean tools. Emiliani thinks that Real Lean cannot be implemented unless leaders and employees are prepared to challenge the status quo (Figure 5.1).

Individualized resistance is expressed as "What is in it for me?"—the question we posed at the start of this section. Answering this requires an appropriate reward structure that shows appreciation and recognition of the extra effort everyone must put in to facilitate change. Rewards do not have to be financial, but they do have to be equitable. People crave genuine acknowledgment of their contributions and often value a simple "Thank-you" or "Well done" more than a financial reward. We discuss rewards in more detail later.

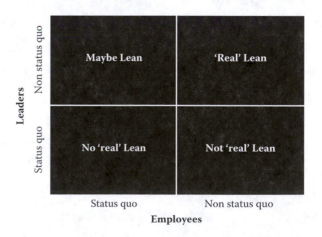

Figure 5.1   Real Lean. (*Source:* Bob Emiliani, *Real Lean – Understanding the Lean Management System,* 2007.)

So what do we mean by *behaviors*? What are the behaviors that we want to encourage, and how do we change people's behaviors?

Lean Behaviors

Examples of Lean behaviors include trust, honesty, openness, consistency, respect, reflection, observation, objectivity, and listening. Wasteful behaviors include blame, ego, distrust, cynicism, sarcasm, ambiguity, subjectivity, insincerity, self-imposed barriers, and negativity.

> Bob Emiliani defines Lean behaviors as "Lean behaviors are simply behaviors that add or create value. It is the minimization of waste associated with arbitrary or contradictory thoughts and actions that leads to defensive behaviors, ineffective relationships, poor co-operation, and negative attitudes." He concludes that "Lean behaviors exhibited by corporate culture should be a strong source of competitive advantage. … Once Lean behaviors are deeply understood, they must be practiced diligently under all conditions until they become sustaining behaviors that replace old habits."

So how do we create Lean behaviors? Well, you can recruit people who exhibit Lean behavior and then you can equip everyone with the right skills through training and development. However, this is not always enough to achieve the right change in culture that is necessary to ensure that the change sticks.

Many years ago, Kurt Lewin, a German psychologist, said that human behavior is a function of both the *person* and the *environment*. He used a mathematical formula to describe this that became known as Lewin's equation:

$$B = f(P,E)$$

This may seem simplistic but it does highlight the point that the work environment plays a big part in encouraging the right behaviors.

So how do you build an environment for sustainable Lean? It involves examining all the elements of the organizational structure with its policies, procedures, measures, and rewards to see if any are acting as roadblocks and stifling progress.

Changing behaviors involves changing the culture of the organization. So let us consider culture for a moment.

Organizational Culture

To make change happen and to embed the changes in an organization, you need to understand the organization and this means understanding its culture.

Two quotes from Edgar Schein's book *Organizational Culture and Leadership* may help you understand the importance of culture when implementing Lean:

Organizational culture is the key to organizational excellence ... and the function of leadership is the creation and management of culture.

Organizational learning, development, and planned change cannot be understood without considering culture as the primary source of resistance to change.

Culture is like the wind. You can feel the strength of it, you can see the effects of it, but there is nothing tangible for you to describe. So we tend to think about culture as the social, moral, and behavioral norms of a group or organization, which are based on the beliefs, attitudes, values, and priorities of the members. The culture of the organization is typically created unconsciously, based on the principles of the top management or the founders of an organization, and it exists where a group of people have been together long enough to have shared problems and have had the opportunity to solve them.

To make any significant organizational change, such as Lean, involves creating the right culture—*a Lean culture*. There is a lot of debate about whether cultures can be managed and deliberately changed. Edgar Schein believes that culture has three levels (Figure 5.2), but it is only at the top two levels that culture can really be changed and managed. These are the values that are strongly influenced by senior management and include the shared beliefs and meanings and the visible artifacts: the symbols, language, and rituals.

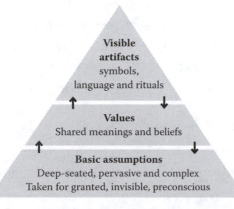

Figure 5.2   Iceberg model of levels of culture and their interaction. (Adapted from Edgar Schein, *Organizational Culture and Leadership*, 2004.)

To facilitate any cultural change, the strategy must be internally consistent with the secondary features of the organization—that is, its design and structure; systems and procedures; the physical layout of the plant; the narratives, myths, and legends about the organization; and the formal expressions of policy and outlook.

Marcel, managing director, was always very aware that changing the culture of the organization would be an essential part of implementing and sustaining change. He started at Schein's top level—the visible artifacts.

He would say to employees, "Look at your environment and ask yourself these questions. Would you be proud to show your family your workplace? Would you dare to show them the rest rooms, the toilets, the canteens?" He says that at first no one would have wanted to show their family around, but they would do so now because it is a nice working environment. He says that they are even working on the outside of the building.

> You can't calculate the return on all of these improvements, so we sold the land we didn't need and used the proceeds to improve the environment, making it a good-looking plant that people can be proud to work at. This is one of our ways for rewarding all their efforts.
> —Marcel, Managing Director, Cogent Power Group

The upgrading of the toilet facilities is symbolic—part of the visible artifacts, but it has demonstrated Marcel's values and his respect for people. The tale has now been passed down as one of the stories that supports the cultural change.

A second symbolic gesture has been the creation of a "Lean Centre." This facility sits in the center of the UK plant and serves as a training center, project room, or meeting room. It is highly visible, a clean and bright new building that has been very well appointed. As a facility, it is impressive; but as a symbol of commitment and seriousness, it is inspirational.

> It is the small things that are extremely important. If you pay attention to these, you get benefits that would be very expensive to acquire. Marcel always gives respect and shows appreciation. There have been tangible and intangible benefits. The mess rooms and personal protective equipment have been improved; people are given the tools to do the job and this is a much better place to work than three years ago.
> —Bill, Divisional Director, Electrical Steels

As well as organizational culture, countries have different national cultures and these can affect the approach and speed of change. Cogent Power has three manufacturing sites: United Kingdom, Canada, and Sweden. Marcel and Frans set the vision and direction but they allowed each site to implement Lean in a way that reflected their different national cultures. Each implementation was therefore different but all were successful.

National Culture

Cultural differences due to national characteristics have been studied by several authors. The best known is probably Geert Hofstede, the author of *Culture and Organizations: Software of the Mind* (2005), who analyzed national cultures on the basis of

- *Power Distance Index (PDI):* The extent to which the less powerful members of organizations accept and expect that power is distributed unequally.
- *Individualism (IDV)* as opposed to collectivism: The degree to which individuals are integrated into groups.
- *Masculinity (MAS)* versus femininity: Refers to the nature of the dominant values, for example, assertiveness, monetary focus, well-defined gender roles, formal structure versus concern for others, focus on quality of relationships, and job satisfaction and flexibility.
- *Uncertainty Avoidance Index (UAI):* Deals with a society's tolerance for uncertainty and ambiguity.
- *Long-Term Orientation (LTO)* versus Short-Term Orientation: Values associated with long-term orientation are thrift and perseverance; values associated with short-term orientation are respect for tradition, fulfilling social obligations, and protecting one's "face."

The Hofstede analyses (Figure 5.3) for Canada and the United Kingdom illustrate their strong feelings about

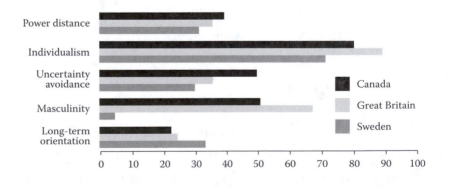

Figure 5.3   Hofstede analysis of Great Britain, Sweden, and Canada. (*Source:* www.geert-hofstede.com.)

individualism and masculinity, indicating a preference for formal structures and a relatively low preference for collectivism. For both countries, long-term orientation ranks lowest, indicating that change can be achieved more rapidly than in many other countries. Compare this to Sweden, which has very low orientation toward masculinity, in line with its consensus culture, and a higher long-term orientation.

The Lean implementation at Cogent Power initially progressed much more slowly in Sweden than in the United Kingdom and Canada. This was because the culture dictated that they discuss everything thoroughly before gaining consensus and approval to take action. However, once they did act, there was a much higher degree of acceptance within the workforce. So the initial pace was slower but more determined.

In contrast, the culture at the Canadian plant was much more entrepreneurial and "have a go" than at either of the European counterparts. Entrepreneurship is widely accepted as part of the business culture of North America, where it is viewed as the process of discovering, evaluating, and exploiting opportunities. Entrepreneurs are characterized by fierce determination and optimism. They usually take a pragmatic approach to problem solving and are willing to take risks to achieve their goals. As a result, they tried more things at the Canadian plant; some worked well, and others were, at best, learning opportunities.

> I supported all kind of investments in Canada. They have that entrepreneurial behavior that I like.
> —Frans, Technology Director, Cogent Power Group

In the United Kingdom, the pace was much smoother, with a steady improvement progression that indicated a more analytical, measured approach reflecting the reserved British culture. Here, pilot projects were very important. They convinced everyone of success prior to roll-out across the plant.

Behaviors are, therefore, part of the cultural systems that are influenced by the visible artifacts and the underlying values and beliefs of the individuals who make up the organization. Let us look now at how we can change behaviors.

Changing Behaviors

So how do you influence Lean behaviors? It starts with *beliefs*. First, you have to believe that something is right for you, and that it is consistent with your own values and the perceived values of the organization. Second, you need the reassurance that the people you respect would behave in a similar fashion. Finally, you have to believe that you have the necessary skills, competencies, and resources to make the change possible. Then you are more likely to behave in a certain way; so beliefs and attitudes drive behaviors.

Behavior is a matter of individual choice and intention. You choose your behavior according to your values, beliefs, and attitudes. The Theory of Planned Behavior (Figure 5.4), developed by Icek Ajzen in 1988, is based on the premise that people do what they intend to do, not what they intend not to do.

Behavioral intention is the antecedent of behavior and is influenced by our attitudes, the opinions of people

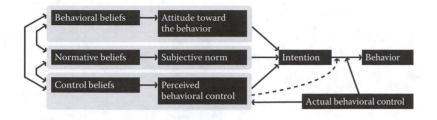

Figure 5.4 Theory of planned behavior (Icek Ajzen). (Adapted from http://www.people.umass.edu/aizen/tpb.diag.html ©2006 Icek Ajzen.)

we respect, and whether we believe in our own ability. Jo Beale, a former colleague at Cardiff University, has applied the Theory of Planned Behavior to Lean implementations and has shown that communication and training are effective intervention mechanisms that affect an employee's willingness to adopt Lean behaviors (Figure 5.5).

People perform better when they know the reasons why change is necessary. One of the keys to gaining an employee's motivation for change is communication. Employees need to be made aware of the reason for introducing the Lean approach within their organization, what outcomes can be expected, and what role they will play in the new organization. Effective two-way communication can serve to include workers in the change program, to give them a sense of ownership of the changes taking place, and to foster an open and democratic environment.

> I believe in direct communication and giving people orientation. I've always started by presenting the output of what the change can be, so that people are aware of the bigger picture of what's going on, and I believe in being very, very open in communication.

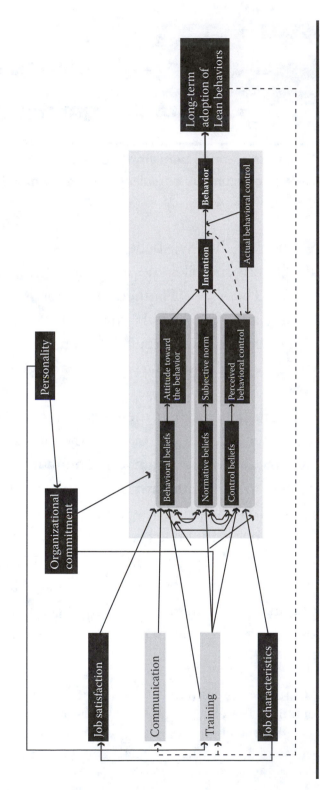

Figure 5.5   People-centered Lean sustainability model. (Adapted from Jo Beale and Peter Hines, 2007.)

> We had about twelve sessions to groups of 100 to 200 people involving the whole workforce, presenting our objectives and how we could improve our performance, and then we had Q and A sessions. ... So no glossy magazines telling people how good everything is. It was just me, telling the truth.
> —Marcel, Managing Director, Cogent Power Group

In December 2003, Marcel held a two-day meeting at Mathern Palace, in South Wales (it is not as grand as it sounds!). He invited all the senior managers from all plants. At this meeting he announced his intention to turn Cogent Power into a Lean organization. For many, this was their first introduction to Lean, so he had external consultants to take them through a Lean awareness session. This meeting has gone down in the Cogent history as "The Mathern Palace Meeting" that effectively kick-started the Lean transformation.

Early in the journey, Cogent Power embarked on a comprehensive Lean coach training and development program. This training was in theory and practice but with more emphasis on the latter. The coaches were selected mainly from inside the organization, and these volunteers were chosen for their experience in manufacturing, sales, technical, and engineering disciplines. The coach program offered both theoretical and hands-on tools and techniques training. The coaches were supported by the local management teams, and the focus of their improvement activity was aligned with the business strategic and operational priorities. During the first phase of the journey, the business carried out two externally facilitated Lean coach programs and also began internal education at the plant level. Employees who demonstrated a willingness to participate in the Lean journey were encouraged, and given additional training and responsibility for improvement activities.

At one of the plants, one of the Lean coaches moved on to another position and the plant advertised internally for a replacement. Peter, the HR Director, received 28 applications for the post and made the inspired decision to take them all on. He designed a program that would enable all applicants to spend time out of their positions working with the formally trained Lean coaches. After a three-month period, they would return to their position with the title of Support Coach and the added responsibility of supporting improvement activities in their area.

There is no set recipe for the structure and set-up of any Lean coach community other than the selected team must best represent the situational needs of the organization. In plants where people culture is critical, consider a variety of options (such as support coaches) to better engage and motivate people at all levels of the organization.

Frans and Peter were heavily involved in the Lean coach program. Frans was appointed by Marcel as the Lean maestro and given operational responsibility. Frans took a very hands-on approach and arranged quarterly "Quo Vadis?" networking sessions. "Quo Vadis?" literally means "Where are you going?" or "Where do we go from here?" These sessions were formal review and direction-setting meetings that involved all the Lean coaches from all sites.

The first Quo Vadis session was incredible. We met in Holland. All the Lean coaches were there and we invited Marcel, the Senior Directorate, and General Managers. Marcel opened the meeting in his typically frank style and asked all the coaches to make a presentation on progress. We then split into focus groups. There was a lot of bloodletting with honest feedback and challenge that people were not used to. This made them sit up and think, 'Hey guys—this is for real.'
—Peter, HR Director, Cogent Power Group

It was at one of these meetings that it was recognized that the middle managers had been neglected. The emphasis had been both top-down and bottom-up, leaving the middle managers at a disadvantage. The coaches who had been deployed to help drive the program at Cogent Power became the real leaders of Lean and it was accepted that, in taking a top-down and bottom-up approach to the program, the middle managers had been neglected. They were supposed to be driving change but did not have the same level of Lean skills as the people they were managing. It was evident that they were not owning Lean and therefore not "living the Lean lifestyle," which is so critical to sustainability. This was rectified by designing a specific program— Leading the Lean Lifestyle—that all managers attended and, because Frans and Marcel's leadership was so unremitting, the senior managers gradually realized that this was very different from any earlier change programs and that it involved everyone "living *and* leading the Lean lifestyle."

We have discussed the management group influencing behaviors, but we also need to consider another influential group—the trade unions—and how they were involved in the change.

Involving the Unions

Both the UK and Swedish plants are unionized and the trade unions were involved from the very beginning.

> Right at the beginning we were told and we were given the challenge to convince people that Lean would help secure jobs. It was surprisingly easy; in a very short time we had convinced more people than we thought possible. Some people got involved who were previously 'retired-on-the-job' and they are still involved today.
> —Trade Union Representative, Cogent Power, United Kingdom

When Marcel was announcing his intentions at the Mathern Palace meeting, Peter was communicating the same message to the trade union representatives and shop stewards. Marcel and Peter had discussed the state of the business with them on previous occasions, so it was no surprise to them that something had to change. They had feared that this would mean redundancies and job losses, but Marcel and Peter were quite emphatic that this would not happen as a result of Lean.

Marcel asserted that by improving flexibility and responsiveness to customer demands, Lean would make Cogent Power more competitive. It was up to everyone, including the unions, to make Lean work and turn the company around. It was only by all working together that this could succeed. The strength of Marcel and Peter's conviction persuaded the unions that Lean meant more jobs, not fewer, so they accepted the challenge to help sell Lean to their members.

Initially there were some skeptics who had "seen it all before" and did not expect it to last. But they soon discovered that this was different; it was not going to go away. The trade union (TU) members respected the visible changes that were happening and were impressed by the money that was being spent on training and upgrading facilities such as the toilet and canteen blocks. The investment in the "Lean Centre" demonstrated management's commitment and conviction that Lean was the way forward.

Several of the TU shop stewards later applied to become Lean coaches and, with the management team, became some of the most ardent Lean supporters.

Motivation for Change

Theories of planned behavior draw heavily on expectancy models. These were developed by Victor Vroom and modified later by Lyman Porter and Edward Lawler in *Managerial Attitudes and Performance* (1968). These models (Figure 5.6) recognize that the relationship between employees' behavior at work and rewards is not straightforward. Vroom suggested that employees can be motivated to perform better if they believe that

- Performance relies on effort
- Performance leads to reward
- Rewards are worthwhile

The authors of these models realized that an employee's performance is influenced by factors such as personality, skills, knowledge, experience, and abilities. As a result, people are motivated differently; so when

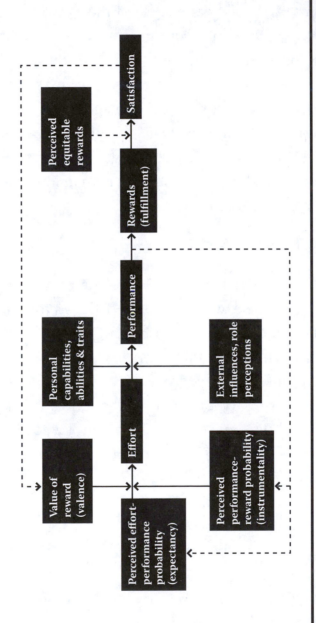

Figure 5.6 Expectancy model. (*Source:* Adapted from Lyman Porter and Edward Lawler, *Managerial Attitudes and Performance*, 2007.)

designing rewards, all these factors must be taken into consideration. Rewards can drive the wrong behaviors, and rewards that are not considered equitable or satisfactory can demotivate rather than motivate. So, care must be taken in the design of rewards. There is a link here to KPIs, which also need to be designed to drive the right behaviors. For example, if employees are rewarded for output, it is pointless to expect them to be motivated to reduce finished goods inventory.

> Motivation is about self-esteem and doing a job well.
> —Peter, HR Director, Cogent Power Group

Peter designed an array of rewards; the first is financial. There is a quarterly bonus scheme that comprises four elements, all directly impacted by Lean improvements. These are measured through KPIs. However, Peter does not just rely on financial rewards, as these do not motivate some people. So to complement the bonus scheme, he introduced other rewards and recognitions. There is a monthly Lean Award Scheme in which individuals are nominated by their managers or peers. The scheme is open to everyone, including full-time contractors. The winning nomination for the Lean Award is decided by the Works Management Council. The winner is entitled to take his or her partner, family, or friends out for a meal at a restaurant of their choice to a value of GBP 100. No money is given in lieu; the winner submits the receipt and the costs are reimbursed. The winner is announced at the monthly trade union meeting and a photograph is taken to be publicized in the Lean Magazine and on the Lean intranet Web site, along with all the other nominations and individual contributions. Employees are also given additional support and training in things that they want to do outside the training required to perform their work-related roles (e.g., car maintenance, DIY, or academic educational subjects). They are entitled to apply for any training course they wish to attend. Attendance for all non-work-related training is outside working time, but all courses will be paid for by the company. The reason for this is that, as people develop new skills, they bring the capacity to learn to work, which increases organizational learning.

Cogent Power also organizes family days where employees' families are invited and shown around the workplace. They are treated to barbecues cooked and served by the managers. All the rewards are designed around the expectancy model in Figure 5.6 to improve performance and increase job satisfaction.

Finally, all employees desire respect, and they thrive where they know that they are valued. You can show respect in many ways: by listening to people, congratulating them, recognizing them, and appreciating them. Encouragement contributes to the success of achieving lasting change. People who are not encouraged tend to lose motivation and give up. Marcel's vision of a self-propelled organization stresses the responsibility of management and leaders to encourage and act on all employee suggestions. This means keeping employees informed, even if the suggestions they make are not considered for action. Once people know the reason why, they can understand and accept decisions. If suggestions are made and nothing further is heard, employees soon become demotivated and lose interest.

Engagement

Between 1995 and 2001, the Gallup organization surveyed over 10 million customers and 200,000 managers. More than 300,000 business units, in hundreds of organizations worldwide, participated in the study. The purpose was to discover what distinguished successful, productive workplaces from those that were not so successful. The results were published in 2004 by Curt Coffman and Gabriel Gonzalez-Molina in *Follow This Path: How the World's Greatest Organizations Drive Growth by Unleashing Human Potential*.

In his foreword to the book, James K. Clifton, CEO of the Gallup organization, states that "The success of your organization does not depend on your understanding of economics, or organizational development or marketing. It depends, quite simply, on your understanding of psychology: how each individual employee connects with

Mike Morrison, Dean of Toyota University, said in an interview with Gabriel Gonzalez-Molina (*Gallup Management Journal*, August 8, 2003):

Lean thinking is best defined as creating organizational wealth. Lean thinking:

Adds value by focusing on customers

Creates flow by focusing on people and processes—and by developing engaged employees who collaborate to engage customers by understanding and anticipating their needs

Achieves mastery by focusing on personal and group learning. This is the final element of Lean thinking. It encompasses one of the most basic human needs: the drive for meaningful growth and progress.

your company: how each individual employee connects with your customers."

Traditionally, organizations have concentrated all their efforts on the things that improve performance: productivity, profits, and growth. They have under-valued the influence of their employees' emotional attachment to the business as a driver of profitability and growth. Toyota is one company that has recognized the value of employee engagement.

The Gallup study found that the biggest differentiator between great and less successful organizations was that great organizations create environments that allow their employees to excel. They also build connections between customers and employees that are emotionally driven. The term that the study used to describe these employees is "emotionally engaged."

However, engaged employees are rare. In 2000, the Gallup organization developed the National Engagement Index. This set out to determine just how large a proportion of the employed population were actually uncommitted to their jobs, which they defined as "emotionally unemployed." The national trend indicates that only about a third of the workplace in the United States is engaged, while approximately a fifth is actively disengaged.

There is a financial cost attached to disengagement. Gallup has calculated that the cost of actively disengaged employees to the U.S. economy is in the range of $253 to $363 billion annually, more than the U.S. budget for defense or education. Just imagine how economies could grow if all employees were engaged with their organizations!

So, if engagement is a win-win situation, how do we go about it?

The Gallup organization has developed a set of twelve conditions that are necessary to create a workplace where employees can become engaged (©The Gallup organization, 2002):

1. Having clearly defined expectations
2. Having the right equipment
3. Being given the opportunity to excel
4. Receiving timely recognition or praise
5. Having line managers that care about you as individuals
6. Being given encouragement to achieve more
7. Having your suggestions and opinions taken seriously
8. Being part of the big picture
9. Having pride in delivering quality output
10. Mutual trust and supportive bonds with other employees and managers
11. Having the opportunity to regularly review progress
12. Having the opportunities to learn and develop

> If you want employees who are involved and engaged, then open, honest, and timely communication is an absolute must.

The first two conditions are the foundations and answer the following questions: What does my job entail? and Do I have the right tools for the job? Conditions 3 through 6 above refer to the care that the employee will receive during his or her employment. Conditions 7 through 10 refer to the environment and each component adds to the other. All are important but none are sufficient on their own to build the right environment; teamwork is essential. Criteria 11 and 12 refer to performance monitoring and development.

One thing that is very clear at Cogent Power is the high level of *employee engagement;* at all the plants, employees comment on the "family atmosphere." This engagement has built up over time and existed before Marcel and Frans arrived. It undoubtedly helped make the transformation easier and more successful. Part of the engagement is down to the age of the plants, particularly in Sweden and the United Kingdom, where the plants are more than 100 years old. Companies of this age often have several generations of employees, and Cogent Power is no exception. It is not unusual to have second or third generations of the same family working there, or having worked there. When this happens, a lot of history builds up that extends beyond the company into the local community. The distinction between work and social leisure becomes blurred as work colleagues participate in local neighborhood teams and community events. Part of the engagement is also down to the work of Peter and other HR managers, in developing the atmosphere of inclusion by holding family barbecues, including families in the Lean Award prizes, and including contractors in the eligibility to apply for awards. It is not just in the older plants that engagement is high. It is also clear at the Canadian plant, a green-field site with many employees who have only been with the company for the past few years. Like behavioral change, communication is the key to engagement. People need to be aware of what needs to change and why. Everyone needs to be told the same story at the same time. Engagement does not wait for the ripple effect as news permeates the company.

Another important mechanism for engagement is *training.* This took place early in the Lean implementation at Cogent Power. The first session was for the senior management, over the course of two days at the Mathern Palace Meeting in December 2003. All the senior managers and divisional directors were given an intense introduction to Lean, covering policy deployment, value stream management, cross-functional teams, and Lean tools. The second phase involved developing and training the Lean coaches. The emphasis here was on "train the trainer." The Lean coaches were equipped with the knowledge and skills to run improvement projects and train others in the Lean concepts and tools. However, as we have seen, the middle managers were not initially involved. They therefore became disengaged and did not get involved in the early stages. As soon as Peter became aware of this, he instigated a Lean leaders training program that all managers attended. To maintain progress and engagement, Peter used the Seven Lean Skills described by Doug Howardell as part of the recruitment and annual appraisal process.

Employees are reviewed formally by their line managers, and their competence in each of the seven skills is assessed. Recently, Peter and the management team introduced another formal process aimed at identifying "blockers." These are employees who knowingly or unknowingly block the improvement progress. The purpose of this process is to address the root cause of the problems and bring them into the open. There are many

1. Customer consciousness
2. Enterprise thinking
3. Adaptation
4. Taking initiative
5. Innovation
6. Collaboration
7. Influence

(Douglas Howardell www.theacagroup.com. © 2004 Doug Howardell, 800.639.7661, Dh@theacagroup.com.)

reasons why someone might block progress: there could be a training need, a capability issue, a resource issue, or some underlying personal reason that needs to be addressed. The "blocker" issues are raised at the management meeting and appropriate action is agreed upon. A manager is assigned to "own" the issue, and it is his or her responsibility to resolve it before the next meeting. This has had a profound effect.

> If someone's behavior or lack of engagement is blocking progress, it needs to be addressed in the same way that any other problem is addressed. This is difficult to take on, but can have extraordinary results.
> —Peter, HR Director, Cogent Power Group

Once individuals are confronted with the problem that results from their behavior, there is always a reaction. Usually the initial reaction is one of hurt or anger. The manager must be very skilled to cope with this as, handled well, the second reaction is generally very positive. The approach is very similar to any other problem diagnosis. The manager needs to collect the data, make sure that it is factual, and then advise the individual, invite a response, and discuss possible solutions. It does require that the managers handling these issues have acquired some pastoral skills. Since its introduction, the effect has been dramatic and, to date, all the "blocker" issues have been resolved and the performance of the individuals completely changed. Peter told us that when one individual was approached and confronted with his actions, he was profoundly hurt but he came back a few hours later and said, "You know what you were saying? I have just realized that you are right." From that point on, his behavior changed and he became totally engaged in the process.

Summary

Nurturing and developing appropriate sets of behavior and establishing high levels of engagement constitute the final element of the "below the waterline" part of our Lean Iceberg. Both of these areas are essential to achieving sustainable Lean change. Indeed, we might go as far as to suggest that making Lean really work is really a people thing. So having the HR community at the center of a Lean transformation is important so that the various people-related policies and procedures encourage rather than inhibit Lean activity. Sadly, this is often not the case and what we see is

- Low levels of engagement—maybe 10 percent
- Assumed high levels of engagement

- Surprise when there is resistance
- Most or all initiatives driven top-down (pushed discontinuous change)
- Little change driven bottom-up (pulled continuous improvement)
- Little or no reflection on past changes
- A lot of wasted opportunities as only a low percentage of people are engaged in the organization's purpose

A quick check: how central are your HR colleagues in your Lean activity? If the answer is "not very," we suggest that you see how this might be changed.

Behavior and engagement learning points can be summarized as follows:

- Lean coaches play a key role in the effective deployment of the Lean program. The early pace of change often depends on the drive and experience of the coach, and therefore the selection of an appropriate Lean coach team is essential.
- The coaches who had been deployed to help drive the program at Cogent Power became the real leaders of Lean, and it was accepted that, in taking a top-down and bottom-up approach to the program, the middle managers had been neglected. It was evident that they were not owning Lean and therefore not "living the Lean lifestyle," which is so critical to sustainability.
- Inject pace into the program using experienced, motivated, and multidisciplined people to form an internal Lean team.

- Encourage sharing and learning throughout the program; take every opportunity to get people together to discuss continuous improvement.
- Lean organizations need Lean people who are both competent and capable of pushing themselves and their teams out of the comfort zone and into the stretch zone.

Use our template (see Figure 8.13c) in Chapter 8 to assess the levels of behavior and engagement in your organization.

III
ABOVE THE WATERLINE

Above the waterline are all the visible features of a Lean implementation. Organizing around key business processes and engaging in process improvement are the cornerstones of a Lean enterprise. Applying Lean tools, technology, and techniques to improve, sustain, and maintain business processes is the route commonly taken by organizations attempting to enhance performance. Visit any Lean organization and you will see examples of process management and the application of Lean tools. Visit any "Real Lean" organization and you will still see process management and Lean tools; what you will not see is all the effort that has been put in below the waterline—to strategy and alignment, leadership, behaviors, and engagement—that sustains the Lean transformation.

This section examines the features of "above the waterline."

Chapter 6

Processes

In *Going Lean: A Guide to Implementation* (2000) we defined key business processes as "patterns of interconnected value-adding relationships designed to meet business goals and objectives." Two things are important when looking at businesses processes.

1. Which processes are key to the core business?
2. How do you design and optimize key processes to deliver value to the customer, business, or value stream?

Each business process comprises a number of steps, tasks, or activities that convert a series of inputs into outputs. Our example (Table 6.1) shows some common processes but you should always define and agree upon your own for your organization.

In our experience, many companies make the mistake of defining too many processes. It is better to settle for between four and ten key business processes that can be defined from start to end.

Many companies find it useful to classify their processes into categories. For example, you might divide the processes into three categories:

Table 6.1   Core business processes.

Key Business Process	Definition
1. Product Lifecycle Management	Managing customer needs for new products. Designing and developing new products, bringing them to market, and retiring obsolete products.
2. Order Creation	Winning new business with existing or new customers.
3. Order Fulfillment	Transforming raw materials into products that meet customer orders including taking orders, order processing, production planning, production, delivery to the customer, and payment management.
4. Technology, Plant and Equipment Management	Developing, managing, and maintaining operating equipment, including IT.
5. Human Resource Management	Developing, managing, and maintaining employees, including training, recruitment, and retention.
6. Strategy and Policy Deployment	The strategic management of the company, focusing on change and management of critical success factors.
7. Supplier Integration and Development	Integrating suppliers into other key business processes, developing new suppliers, and managing supplier relationships.
8. Continuous Improvement	Continuous radical, or incremental, improvement of other key business processes.

1. Processes that focus the overall direction of the organization but do not directly deliver against the targets—strategic processes
2. Processes that directly deliver on top-level targets—core processes

3. Processes that indirectly deliver on top-level targets—support processes

The strategic processes set direction; the core processes, aided by the support processes, deliver the targeted results. Within the core processes, some can be identified as customer facing, such as order fulfillment, order creation, and product life-cycle management. Designing and managing core processes effectively and efficiently ensures that the company can compete and remain competitive.

Our companion book *Going Lean: A Guide to Implementation* (2000) describes how you can select processes to deliver targeted improvements, and we refer you to this for further information.

We believe that improvement in core processes either focuses primarily on waste reduction or, alternatively, on value creation. For example, improving the order fulfillment process is primarily reducing or eliminating waste so as to enhance performance, increase capacity, and reduce cost. Focusing on order creation primarily adds value by generating more sales to utilize excess capacity. Indeed, some people will argue that you cannot create value by increasing sales until you have improved operations and stabilized the process, thus releasing excess capacity. We believe the most effective way is to improve both processes simultaneously; absorbing the excess capacity generated by improvements in processes such as order fulfillment with new sales generated through value-adding processes such as the order creation process.

Why do waste reduction and value enhancement go hand in hand? Waste reduction is often considered a way of reducing costs; after all, waste is costly. But cost is not the only way to compete. Think here about prestige cars, such as Lexus, BMW, or Mercedes-Benz, and compare these to lower-cost alternatives. As well as status, the perceived value of a prestige car is about service, design, or quality. Some processes focus more on adding value, others more on cost reduction. Figure 6.1 demonstrates how this might look.

Consider a product that has slightly above average costs and slightly below average perceived value (point X). Strategically there are a number of options:

1. You could reduce costs and make the product cheaper by reducing all non-value-added activities. The danger of purely reducing costs is that this may not make the product more attractive. Take Rover cars, for example. Cost reduction through job losses alone actually reduced the perceived value (see dotted line in Figure 6.1). Once you are in this position, you are in a continual spiral to keep driving costs down.

2. You could enhance the product to add perceived value. The danger of purely adding value is that, unless you know exactly what the customers value, you might just be adding unwanted features.

3. Removing waste in the order fulfillment process has other benefits, such as improved quality, flexibility, and delivery. So, although this is primarily cost reduction, it might also be value enhancing.

4. Focusing on the order creation process includes understanding customer values. Eliminating activities and transactions that add no value can also reduce costs. So, although primarily value adding, there may also be some cost benefits.

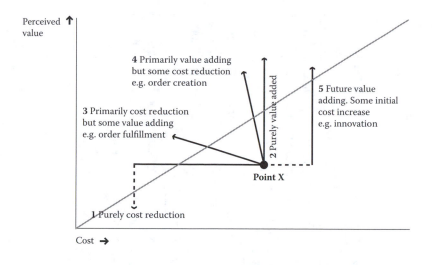

Figure 6.1 Relationships between perceived value and cost.

5. Some processes may incur costs early on; these are "future value adding," such as some innovation processes. Once the new products are developed and sent to market, they can become the focus of further waste reduction and value enhancement.

We believe that you need to focus on both waste reduction and value adding. Let us see why.

Ask yourself the following question: What is the saving from a typical Lean order fulfillment improvement project, such as changing the material flow in a manufacturing cell that reduces the requirement for people by 25 percent? Table 6.2 shows that there are three potential responses.

However, this systematic approach requires expert project management skills and strong cross-functional management to ensure that the additional capacity is released in time to meet the extra sales. Failure to achieve the right balance could lead to a worsening on-time

Table 6.2 Potential responses to savings in direct labor requirements as a result of Lean improvements.

Scenario	What We Hear	What It Means	Longer Term Result
1	We have saved 25% of direct labor costs as we have made a quarter of our shop floor staff in the cell redundant.	We have unwittingly disengaged our workforce and almost certainly removed the opportunity for future successful improvement.	Lean has become synonymous with job cuts and has created shop floor opposition.
2	We have saved 25% of direct labor costs from the shop floor cell as we have moved these people 'somewhere else'.	In most cases this means that there has been no real cost savings as "somewhere else" does not imply increasing output.	Firms fail to realize real benefits from the application of Lean thinking as they focus on savings that are all too often unreal.
3	We have reinvested the 25% of people who were freed up in 2 new business in another area where new work has been brought in to the business.	The benefit of the freed up people has been multiplied by getting them to work on new business with their "free" labor.	A multiplier effect is produced when Waste Removing and Value Creating processes work in tandem that greatly enhances the benefits and results in profitable growth.

delivery performance and customer satisfaction, with a consequent loss of repeat new orders.

Although much of the early focus at Cogent Power was on getting stability in the order fulfillment process, there was also some initial Lean work with commercial departments to standardize the order creation process. Mindful of the first Lean principle—*understanding value from the customer's perspective*—Cogent Power began engaging key customers at the outset, discussing the basic value requirements in terms of quality, cost, and delivery of both products and service.

Capturing the "voice of the customer" and understanding customer value clearly is fundamental to Lean, but it is often missed by companies that concentrate on implementing Lean tools. The voice of the customer (VOC), as you will see later, features at three points in the order creation process: setting the marketing vision, generating new business, and retaining existing clients.

In this chapter we concentrate on Cogent Power's experience in developing two core processes—order fulfillment and order creation—as examples of waste reduction and value creation.

Eliminating Waste in the Order Fulfillment Process

The removal of waste both inside and between companies is fundamental to a Lean system. To eliminate waste, you must first learn to see waste; put on your *muda* glasses.

When thinking of waste, consider the activities within an organization. There are three types of activity:

1. *Value-adding:* Activities that, in the eyes of the customer, add value to a product or service. These are activities that are not wasteful and are part of the product or service that the customer is happy to pay for. Some of these may create future value-add, such as new products.

2. *Non-value-adding:* Activities that, in the eyes of the customer, add no value to a product or service. These activities are clearly wasteful and should be the target for immediate removal.

3. *Necessary, but non-value-adding:* Activities that, in the eyes of the customer, do not add value to a product or service but are necessary at the present time to deliver the product or service to the customer. These activities should be the target for future improvement, or longer-term radical change.

In the physical environment (manufacturing or logistics flow), the ratio between the various activities is commonly

■ 5 percent value-added
■ 60 percent non-value-added
■ 35 percent necessary, but non-value-added

This looks poor; but in an information flow environment (e.g., office, distribution, or retail), the ratio is commonly

■ 1 percent value-added
■ 49 percent non-value-added
■ 50 percent necessary, but non-value-added

So there is generally considerable scope for improvement. Let us now see how Cogent Power went about identifying waste and removing it from the order fulfillment process.

Identifying Waste in the Order Fulfillment Process

Order fulfillment is the complete process from the point-of-sales inquiry to delivery of a product or service to the customer. It includes order processing, production, inventory and materials management, logistics, shipment, and distribution. The scope of the order fulfillment process ultimately includes the whole supply chain, from raw material suppliers to end customers.

Before you can eliminate waste, you need to be able to identify it. One way of doing this is to map the current state of the process and get a visual picture of the physical and information flows. This will highlight where the flow is disrupted by detours, backflows, waiting, or scrap.

The technique they used at Cogent Power was *big picture mapping*. This is described in detail in *Learning to See* by Rother and Shook (1998), and the reader is referred to this and other texts on mapping, such as our earlier books, *Going Lean: A Guide to Implementation* (2000) and *Lean Profit Potential* (2002).

The key to any process mapping is to be clear on the end-to-end process; this is where your definitions come in. Start by mapping one value stream, but always be conscious that processes can contain more than one value stream and resources can be shared across the value streams. Before you start, choose a value stream that is important to the business, such as a key product line to a key customer or market segment.

Senior management needs to select the key value streams within order fulfillment that are aligned to the strategy as the foci for improvement.

Big picture mapping is a useful tool borrowed from Toyota. It will

- Help you visualize the flows
- Help you see where the waste is
- Pull together the Lean thinking principles
- Help you decide who should be on the implementation teams
- Show relationships between information and physical flows
- Create buy-in from the senior team undertaking the big picture mapping

There is nothing like walking the process and talking to people as they work to find out how the value actually flows from customer order to delivery.

Big picture mapping is a five-phase process. But forget the dusty procedure manuals; in this, and other value stream mapping tools, it is important to record what *actually* happens, not what is *supposed* to happen.

Most waste can be found in the workarounds that have become custom and practice.

The tools and resources you need include

- A cross-functional mapping team, which includes some senior people to give it authority, and some direct employees, shop floor or office based, who can give it depth of knowledge
- Large sheets or rolls of brown paper
- Colored pens or pencils
- Colored Post-it notes

Phase 1 Start by collecting all the information on customer demand for the product or products you are mapping:
- What is the customer demand or how many products are wanted and when?
- How many different parts are made?
- What is the delivery pattern? How many? How often? Any special information (e.g., multiple delivery points, delivery windows).
- What packaging is required?
- How much stock does the customer hold?

Phase 2 Map the information flow:
- What sort of forecast and call-off information is supplied by the customer?
- Who (or which department) does this information go to in your firm?
- How long does it stay there before being processed?

– What sort of forecast and call-off information do you give your suppliers?

– What order quantities do you specify?

Phase 3 Map the physical product flow:

– What is the pattern of raw material supplies? How often and how much is delivered?

– How much raw material stock do you hold?

– For each step in the process, record:

• How long it takes to process (i.e., the cycle time)

• The number of people who are involved

• How long it takes to set up and change over between parts (i.e., changeover time)

• The batch size

• How long the product waits before it passes to the next stage (i.e., the WIP inventory)

– How much finished goods stock do you hold?

Phase 4 Link the information flow with the physical flow:

– What sort of scheduling information is used?

– What sorts of work instructions are produced?

– Where is the information and instruction sent from and to?

– What happens when there are problems in the physical flow?

Phase 5 Add a timeline:

– Record the value-adding component of the total production lead-time to complete the map.

At Cogent Power, they used big-picture mapping (Figure 6.2) to map the order fulfillment process for critical products or key customers at all the plants, and these maps formed the basis of the improvement projects. The best way of viewing current state maps is not on the screen of a PC but on a large sheet of brown paper on the wall of a prominent office or project room, where the whole mapping team and senior managers can gather and discuss what they see.

Once you have mapped the current reality, it should be easy to identify where waste is accumulating and causing disruptions in the flow. These should be marked on brightly colored Post-it notes as they will be the focus of future improvement projects.

> The application of value stream mapping tools needs to focus on longer-term management, not just mapping.
> Don't be a "happy mapper" who never gets past just doing mapping exercises.

From Current State to Future State

It is all very well to identify waste in the current state, but this alone will not give you any improvement. The next step is to create a picture of the process once all the non-value-adding steps have been eliminated and then identify the tasks that you have to complete to realize this. These are called "future, or ideal state maps."

It is possible that there are a number of future states that you have to develop before you can reach the ideal state (Figure 6.3).

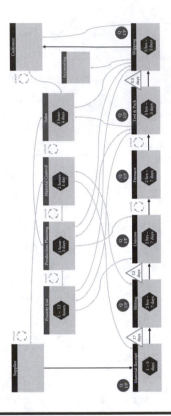

Figure 6.2 Current state map.

From the current state map, Cogent Power developed an initial ideal future state map (Figure 6.4) that took out virtually all of the non-value-adding waste. To achieve this, they had to make major changes, which did not happen all at once. They had to identify many projects that would form the road map to get them from the current to the ideal future state. They also had to reorganize the structure and performance metrics, and involve suppliers and customers.

The senior management teams of the plants reviewed the profit potential of the various value streams and, based on volumes, margins, and future growth criteria, were able to select the key areas of focus for the

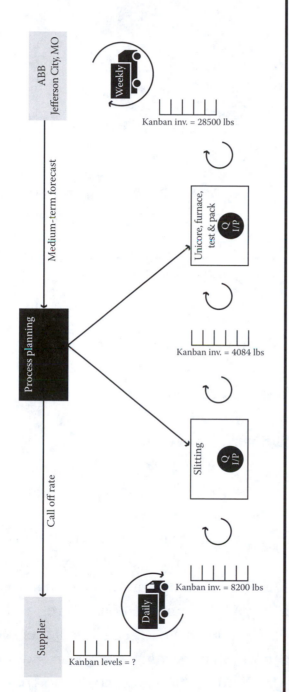

Figure 6.3   Future state map.

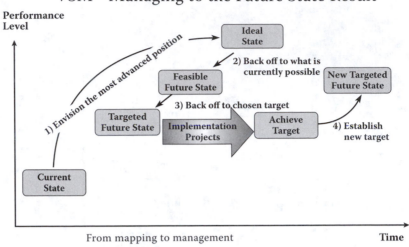

Figure 6.4   Managing the future state.

operating teams to work on. The business imperative for one of the chosen value streams included

- Improving on-time delivery
- Reducing space
- Reducing internal stock
- Reducing supplier stock-outs
- Reducing customer lead-times

The ideal future state map is very much simpler than the old current state and uses technology in an innovative way. However, creating future state maps is not a one-off exercise. As the organization evolves and learns, it must revisit the future state to see if it still meets expectations. Organizational learning takes place during the transformation. Future states that could not have been imagined early on become feasible as the transformation progresses.

In Canada, one of the things they had to do was replace the old hierarchical, functional system with a new cross-functional team. They replaced the single operations manager role with four new roles: three reporting to the operations director and the fourth to the commercial director. The new roles were

- Materials manager—responsible for all material supplies to the whole process.
- Two production managers—each responsible for separate production processes, acting as internal customers and suppliers.
- Order fulfillment manager—responsible for overseeing the whole process from customer order to customer satisfaction.

As well as the management team, Cogent Power also developed a new team leader structure to provide the needed leadership at the shop-floor level. This has been one of the keys to long-term sustainability.

Improvements in the order fulfillment process will not be maximized unless the excess capacity is converted into extra sales. So, once operations had started to improve, Cogent Power turned their attention to adding value in the order creation, or sales, process to take advantage of the additional spare capacity.

Adding Value in the Order Creation (Sales) Process

Order creation comprises two business functions: sales and marketing. Within the process, each function has different roles and responsibilities. However, what we frequently see in business is trench warfare between the sales and marketing functions, each trying to control the other. Within order creation we are combining them in a seamless strategic and operational process.

Order creation adds value by generating more sales. These sales are required to create the profit potential multiplier effect by soaking up the extra people, equipment, and space capacity created primarily by waste-removing processes such as order fulfillment.

Like order fulfillment, improving a sales process starts by understanding the current state of the process. This means putting on the *muda* glasses again and identifying waste. However, here we are in an information-based environment, so we need to reinterpret the seven wastes as in Figure 6.5.

The sales process can be described as a five-phase process that might look something like the one shown in Figure 6.6. This illustrates both winning new business and generating repeat business. You can see that the Lean term "Voice of the customer" (VOC) sits within phases 1 (Setting the direction), 4 (Selling in), and 5 (Selling on).

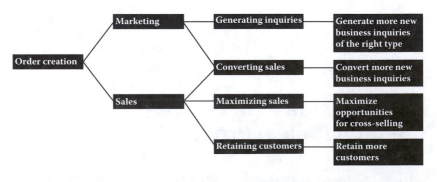

Figure 6.5   Order creation.

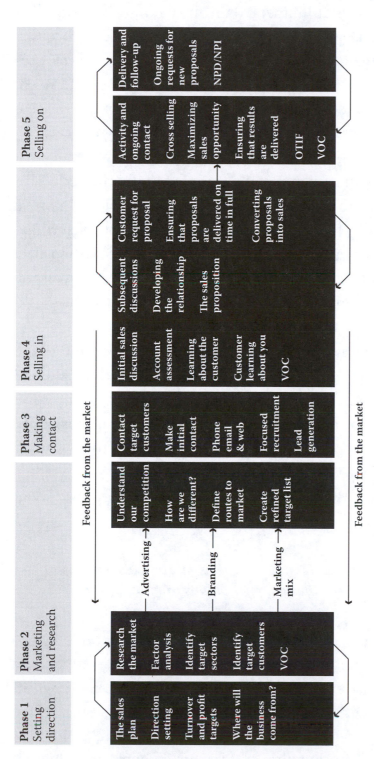

Figure 6.6   Phases of the order creation process.

As in order fulfillment, there are a number of tools that you can use to map and understand the sales process.

The main purpose of mapping processes is to produce a visual representation of the current state to make it easier to identify disruptions in the flow of the process so that these can be removed or reduced.

Another purpose is to determine the baseline so that improvements can be measured and monitored. This helps sustain the effort and encourages people to improve continually. In the sales process, it is useful to determine a value for each stage in the process. From existing data on inquiries, you can calculate the rate for converting inquiries to sales; and by looking at repeat orders, you can determine a rate for customer retention.

By examining all the data and brainstorming the issues and opportunities, you can develop realistic and timely targets for a future state map. In order to improve, you need to understand how and why your performance levels are operating at a certain level and then start to remove the waste.

But first there is one important question to ask about removing waste from a system:

> *How can you remove waste from a process unless you know what the customer values from that process?*

The answer to this is that you cannot, so understanding customer value becomes very important, particularly in the customer-facing business processes. As shown in the following illustration, understanding customer value informs strategy and other processes, such as innovation and product life-cycle management. In addition, customer value analysis is a separate activity that runs simultaneously with the sales process mapping to feed into the future state maps, forming the basis for improvement projects.

Let us now look at understanding the voice of the customer and see how this helped Cogent Power change the face of its business. Later we will look at an example of mapping how orders are created.

Understanding the Voice of the Customer

Integral to Cogent Power's success was the recognition that it needed to put into practice the first principle of Lean. The organization needed to understand the voice of the customer and, with the improvements in order fulfillment, it was now in a position to do something about it.

> In common with traditional businesses, customer value was initially perceived as merely quality, cost, and delivery (QCD), and the business had not yet really captured the true voice of the customer.

The problem is that there is little written in the Lean textbooks about how to capture the voice of the customer and, although this is seen as the first Lean principle, 90 percent of companies applying Lean will do little or no customer survey work and immediately jump into mapping and applying Lean tools. Indeed, we often ask our students and partner companies to name Womack and Jones' four Lean principles, as the first, "Specify customer value," is so rarely seen in practice!

The Lean term "voice of the customer" is an interesting concept. In practice there are two distinct components:

1. *Pre-ordering:* where the suppliers need to listen and then demonstrate that they have heard and understood the things that are important to the customer, the value criteria.
2. *Post-delivery:* which is about the level of customer satisfaction achieved. Did the product or service offered meet expectations, exceed them, or fall below them?

Imagine you are a customer for a defined product or service. You may have a number of potential suppliers willing and able to supply you:

Part 1: You may have a number of *criteria* that are important to you and that you would *value* and look for in relation to the supply of that product or service; these are called your *value criteria*.

Part 2: At the same time (and it would most probably remain unspoken), you would also *measure the performance* of the supplier against these *value criteria* and also against your *expectations* based upon your past experiences. This measure of performance versus expectations would be rated as a level of *customer satisfaction*.

If you verbally told your supplier what it was that you valued and looked for with respect to these value criteria and also how the supplier was performing with respect to these value criteria and against your expectations, the supplier would be hearing the "voice of the customer."

Although the suppliers might "hear" what you are saying, they may choose "not to listen" in the truest sense and might not amend the offering to meet your specific requirements. In any event, as a customer you will place your business (or repeat business) with the supplier who best demonstrates a deep understanding of your specific needs and aligns their offering accordingly.

Both parts of the voice are measurable and should inform all other key processes, including strategy, innovation, order creation, and even the people development processes.

Many companies fall into the trap of believing that they know what their customers really value—in reality, a large number actually do not know. In most customer-supplier relationships, suppliers know who the key decision makers are within their customer's operation. Importantly, surprisingly few actually have an accurate fix on the influencers of the buying decision, and that these people have value criteria that need to be heard and understood.

True customer satisfaction is only really achieved when a supplier consistently meets or exceeds their customer's expectations measured against a range of their customer's value criteria.

> During recessionary periods, suppliers should stay even closer to their Customers—they will guide you through the troubled periods and let you know what you have to do to continue to win their business.
> —Richard Harrison

There are usually more people in an organization who influence the buying decision than is realized. These people are touchpoints in the process. Really understanding the range of value criteria at all the key touchpoints, and being able and willing to respond, is a differentiating factor that companies need to recognize.

When they first started Lean at Cogent Power, it was little different than in most companies. According to Chris, the divisional director,

> We started with customer surveys and I have to be honest about this, I made a complete and total mess of it when I first started. I went out to our biggest customers and I came back really with a hodge-podge of stuff. There was nothing that we were able to collate, correlate, or observe. Things like 'We don't like your delivery,' etc. Richard Harrison came out and we got going on the [order creation] process and started talking about the voice of the customer. I shared my experience with him and he said, 'Let's look at the survey again,' and, in the end he showed us how to do it, with the appropriate people in place; not just them and me sitting in front of each other, with them looking at the time, wondering how long it was going to take and when it would be over.

The first thing that Richard said to Chris was, "You want to improve the process. Okay, first let us do a survey to get the voice of the customer and then I'll be back to analyze the order creation process."

At Cogent Power they used the survey to help them really understand customer value.

The survey team initially consisted of three people:

■ The relationship holder, Chris, already had a number of contacts and his primary role was to manage customer expectations throughout the project.

- The Lean Manager, Greg, acted as a "Lean standard." His job was to run the interviews and ask all the questions in a set pattern. Greg received specialist neuro-linguistic programming (NLP) interview training to help him discover exactly what the customers really valued.

- The Cogent Power team also decided to take along an engineering specialist. His job was to help record the information given by the customers and to investigate any technical issues.

The Canadian plant selected 17 key customers and conducted 130 face-to-face interviews. Each interview lasted approximately an hour. The interviews set out to understand the customer values at different touchpoints and specifically what "good service" looks or feels like against each of the values. The team did all the interviews face to face with a targeted cross-section from their customers.

- They identified the individual value criteria from each person interviewed.
- They ranked the values in terms of importance to the customers.
- For their existing customers, they measured their own performance against the customers' expectations.
- They explored the future in terms of where the market and supply chains where going.
- They explored additional areas of "value-add" that they could offer their customers.
- Finally, they asked the customers to sum up their experience of dealing with them as a supplier.

The team quickly made some very interesting and exciting discoveries:

- Many of the things they were doing were right; they just needed to do more of them and release time from activities that were not adding value from their customers' perspectives.
- Despite having supplied customers for many years and having thought that they knew the real influencers, they did not.
- Many of their customers wanted to have more advanced proactive partnerships.
- The nearer to the shop floor they conducted the interviews, the more quick wins they discovered that they were able to act on.

According to Chris and Greg, the response from customers was fantastic. Chris told us,

> We interviewed 130 people across 17 customers. I was a bit concerned that all of these guys would want to talk to us, that it wasn't personal enough, but in fact the opposite was true. It was, 'You are a very special person, and here is your day.' Even the coolest characters opened up after five or ten minutes. As a result, the information that we got from our customer base was fantastic. We went and put money into some key areas. We couldn't do everything, but we are working through it.

Conducting the Survey

The first step is to identify all the touchpoints, all of those people who, in some way, come into contact with the product or service. This is maybe one of the managers, the buyer, the materials handlers, invoice clerks, or shop-floor operators who process the products. At Cogent Power they identified up to eighteen touchpoints per customer.

The first step is to ask each interviewee what constitutes value from their individual perspective. This determines the customer value criteria against which your product or service will be assessed. The second step is to ask them to rate how you perform against their expectations; how you perform against the competition; and finally, how you perform against the best supplier of any product or service with which they come into contact. Figure 6.7 provides an example of the survey conducted by Cogent Power.

Once all the responses have been collated and summarized, the scores for each category can be used to calculate an overall customer perception index. The majority of Cogent Power's customers cited quality as one of their most important value criteria. Conducting the survey helped Cogent Power drill down to explore the perceptions of quality in detail. This produced some surprising results and identified twenty-two design- and engineering-related issues (Figure 6.8), some of which were very easily remedied. For example, many customers criticized the way products were labeled. Changing this was straightforward, and it delighted customers.

Other issues were more complex, and these were fed into the strategy review process. However, response to all the issues raised was fed back to the customers to keep them informed.

Voice of the Customer Survey

Customer Value Criteria	Against Expectations			Against Competitor			Against Best Overall		
	Better Than	Same As	Worse Than	Better Than	Same As	Worse Than	Better Than	Same As	Worse Than
Pricing	xx	x		x	xx		x	xx	
Quality		xxx		xx	xx		x	xx	x
Customer Service	x	xx	x	xx	xx			xx	x
Technical Support		x					x		
Communication		xx		x			x		
Delivery		x	x		xx	x		x	xx
Environment		x		x					x
Partnership	xx		x	xx	x	x	x	xx	x
Packaging	x	xx		xx			x		x
Safe Handling			x		x				x

Figure 6.7 Customer survey template.

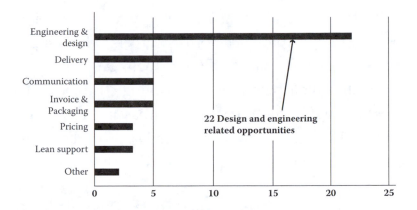

Figure 6.8 Voice of the customer summary of the follow-up opportunities.

Managing customer expectations is very important when considering a survey like this. Not all suggestions can be turned into actions at first but it is essential that, where they can be, they are. Customers will soon lose interest if they see no improvement, and this can easily turn a reasonably well-satisfied customer into a very dissatisfied one.

So two things are necessary: (1) that there is top-level commitment and support for the process, and (2) that customers are told honestly and up-front that some suggestions will have to be postponed if the finances or resources are not available immediately. The important point is that the communication is open and honest, and that people are kept informed.

> When we really got going, doing these customer surveys was one of the best experiences that I have had in my personal career. One of the reasons was that we went right to the very top, straight to the presidents and left them with little doubt about what we're doing here with our Lean implementation.
>
> —Chris, Divisional Director, Canada

As Chris said, conducting the survey was one of the most satisfying experiences of his career. Other employees also reported that it opened their eyes and made them realize their own role in satisfying customers. This served to engage the commercial areas in Lean as they could see how the program impacted improved customer relationships and additional business.

> One of our customers invited some of the suppliers to a meeting to explain that they were implementing Lean. I was a key supplier, so I spent two days with them. They had spent a ton of money bringing in this Japanese sensei. And they went out and Kaizen Blitzed the place over two days and they were all cheering. I sat in on the presentation, and somewhere through the process I had spoken to the vice president and I wanted to share with him a bit of our experiences, which were a little bit different. I was trying to explain that we had done it differently, that we had gone through the strategy and all our managers understood the strategy. But he was not going to hear some small company from Canada that he'd never heard of telling him how to do things. There is no chance in the world that this company has the faintest clue what the customer really wants, none at all, none whatsoever; they are not set up to do this. Don't get me wrong, there's nothing wrong with Kaizen Blitz but don't attach that to Lean or sustainability.
>
> —Chris, Commercial Director, Canada

The feedback indicated that there was a real market opportunity for the business to grow into new but aligned markets where they did have expert knowledge. Traditionally, the business had supplied quality component parts to other manufacturers; but Cogent Power's end users were indicating that there was now a real opportunity for the business to add value to their existing products by moving up the "value ladder" and developing a higher-quality engineered product and service at a competitive price.

The improvements they had made in order fulfillment had created excess capacity and this gave them the opportunity to "in-source" part of the value-adding activity from their customers at little extra cost. The result of this was that they could profitably grow the Cogent Power business at the same time as shortening the supply chain to their customers, reducing the threat from competition in what is traditionally a mature, highly competitive, price-sensitive marketplace.

Mapping the Sales Process

The sales process can be mapped just like any other. Mapping enables the manager to identify key areas of non-value-added activity and waste that can then be removed.

In another example at Cogent Power, they mapped a sales process using a technique called *four fields mapping*. Four fields mapping is a useful technique for process mapping, particularly for information flows; it identifies the *What, Who, Why,* and *How* of a process in four fields:

■ Field 1 breaks the process into phases and takes into account the phases that the process goes through. This defines the *What* of a process.

- Field 2 identifies the stakeholders that are involved and defines the *Who* of a process.
- Field 3 recognizes the criteria, or standards, that must be met and defines the *Why*.
- Field 4 maps and describes the activities that take place, the *How* of the process.

Some companies also use two more fields: time elapsed and resource time taken. As each phase is being mapped, it is useful to capture the issues and opportunities for improvement on Post-it notes and then transfer them to flipcharts to form the basis of the future state improvement plan. These become the focus for improvement.

Four fields mapping was used early on at Cogent Power to map some processes, but a new mapping tool was developed to handle the complexity of the sales process. This mapping tool listed all the defined steps and the issues and concerns, as well as the stakeholders. For each problem or issue, the root cause is identified and categorized as a process or a cultural issue.

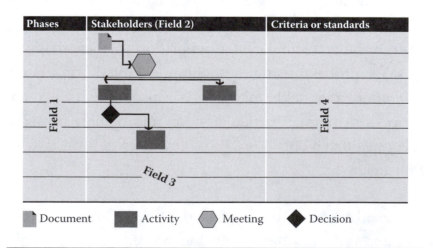

Figure 6.9   Four fields mapping.

Future state mapping of the sales process should take a standard approach so that all five phases of the sales process (Figure 6.6) are covered; in this way the whole process is optimized, rather than just individual elements.

Summary

Process Management: What we often find is

- People work on the four Lean principles.
- There is a lot of functional conflict at all levels.
- 90-plus percent of companies only work on order fulfillment.
- There is rarely any attempt to even identify key business processes.
- 90-plus percent of companies assume "Lean = Reduce Cost" only.
- There are a lot of wasted opportunities as people tend to only try to improve their own silo area, often causing problems for others.

In many businesses, sales are seen as a department rather than as a process. In reality, the order creation process is just like any other process in the business: order fulfillment, new product development, etc.

It is very often the case that salespeople, who have a specific set of skills, are not always clear process thinkers. They miss out on the ability to improve performance by looking at sales as an activity through a different set of lenses.

Because of this, there is very often a feeling in commercial departments that the principles of Lean, being applied in other parts of a business, simply do not apply to them.

The ability to think about order creation as a process with distinct phases means that the process can be analyzed more easily to identify strengths and weaknesses.

Measures and targets can be aligned across the process and, equally as important, the business can start to join up processes as part of the whole value stream that is seen through the eyes of the customer.

Cogent Power themselves initially exhibited all these traits and then undertook a detailed review of their order creation process that changed the face of the business.

The process management learning points can be summarized as follows:

- The application of value stream mapping tools needs to focus on longer-term management, not just mapping.
- Senior management needs strategically to select the key value streams that need sustained improvement focus.
- Continuously apply customer value analysis to inform and improve all other key business processes.
- Apply the VOC process rigorously to really understand the range of value criteria at key touchpoints within the organization. Be able and willing to respond to and align with those needs to differentiate your business from the competition and build long-term business relationships.

■ Distinguish between understanding value criteria and delivering customer satisfaction, and use the data to inform all the key internal and external processes and therefore build an end-to-end Lean, profitable, and sustainable business model.

Use our template (see Figure 8.13d) in Chapter 8 to assess how well the processes are managed in your organization.

Chapter 7

Technology, Tools, and Techniques

Technology, tools, and techniques (TTT) comprise the fifth element of our Sustainable Lean Iceberg—and the last; this is deliberate. Tools should be driven by the needs of the customer, the business, and the people within the business; they should be *pulled*, not *pushed*. Nothing better demonstrates the different approaches that the three Cogent Power plants have taken than the way technology, tools, and techniques have been applied. Marcel and Frans were not prescriptive in how Lean was to be applied; they simply provided the education, resources, and inspiration. In this section we draw on the wealth of literature surrounding this area and illustrate it with examples taken from the real-life application at the various plants.

This chapter is not meant to be an exhaustive description of all the tools and techniques. For detailed discussion, we refer you to some of the excellent texts on the subject: for example, *The Lean Toolbox: Essential Guide to Transformation (4th edition)* by Bicheno and Holweg.

We start this chapter with an overview of the Lean tools and techniques and then concentrate on how Cogent Power used Lean TTT to

- *Manage* a Lean environment
- *Operate* a Lean environment
- *Sustain* a Lean environment

First, however, we take a general look at the Lean tools and techniques. We end this chapter with a few words about the technologies.

Lean Tools and Techniques: An Overview

Previous chapters on strategy and alignment, leadership, behaviors and engagement, and process management discussed some of the Lean tools and techniques to illustrate Cogent Power's journey already. Let us review these here (Table 7.1).

In this chapter we bring the Lean tools, technologies, and techniques together and illustrate them with examples from Cogent Power.

One way is through the toyota production system (TPS) House Model developed by Taiichi Ohno and Eiji Toyoda in the 1950s to explain Toyota's system to employees and suppliers. The TPS House comprises two pillars of Just-in-Time and Jidoka (automation with a human touch). The house is supported by solid foundations, represented by stability and standardization, and is maintained and improved through iterations of continuous improvement, or kaizen, following PDCA, or the

Table 7.1 Lean tools, techniques and technologies discussed in earlier chapters.

Section	Lean Tools And Techniques
Strategy and Alignment	Policy Deployment/Hoshin Kanri
	A3 Planning and Storyboards
	Catchball
	PDCA
	Visual Management
Leadership	Lean Leadership
Behaviors and Engagement	7 Lean Skills
	Team Cultures
	Lean Coaches
	Continuous Improvement
Process Management	Big Picture Mapping
	Four Fields Mapping
	Pull Systems
	Voice of the Customer Insight Tool

scientific method. At the heart of the TPS are the people—those flexible, motivated employees who continually strive for perfection.

In *Andy and Me: Crisis and Transformation on the Lean Journey*, Pascal Dennis, a former engineer at Toyota Motor Manufacturing Canada, shows where the Lean tools and techniques fit within the TPS house. As you can see from the illustration in Figure 7.1, some of the tools and techniques apply across many areas (for example, 5S, Visual Management, kanbans, and problem solving).

Earlier we looked at identifying waste and using maps for recognizing areas for improvement. Before we go on to discuss the tools, let us look at the approaches we can take to implement them. We term this the pillars or platform approach (Figure 7.2).

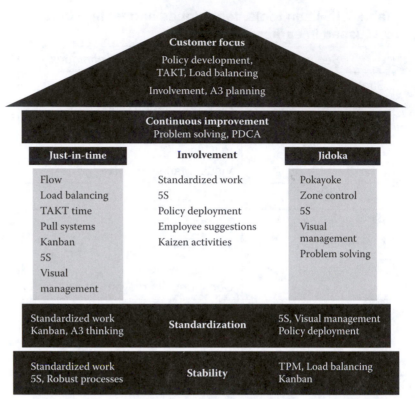

Adapted from *Andy & Me: Crisis and Transformation on the Lean Journey*
by Pascal Dennis

Figure 7.1   Lean tools and techniques. (*Source:* Pascal Dennis, *Andy & Me: Transformation on the Lean Journey*, Productivity Press, 2005.)

A *pillar approach* typically takes one or more steps in the process and applies several Lean tools or techniques, such as 5S, Visual Management, standard operating procedures (SOPs), and kanban, to improve it. The benefit of this approach is that you can quickly demonstrate the benefits of the tools and you can use this to pilot improvements. Pilots generate involvement and belief, so they have a vital role in any change program. But there is a danger in developing pilots into "pillars of excellence," as this can lead to employees

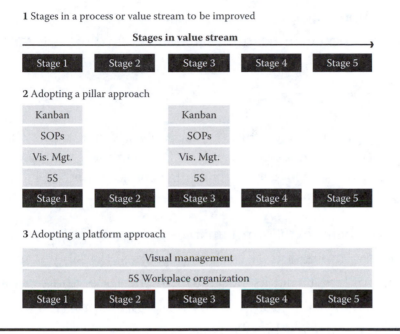

Figure 7.2   Pillars or Platform approach to Lean transformation.

in the unimproved areas feeling isolated and becoming disengaged from the program. Sometimes, this approach can also have a negative effect on the employees in the improved areas who wonder why they are being asked to change when others are left to their own devices, particularly if these employees think that they are being asked to work harder.

> Pilots are very important to convince people, you have to demonstrate and give them the confidence. With confidence they can do anything.
> —Frans, Technology Director, Cogent Power Group

An alternative approach is what we term a *platform approach*. In this, a small number of tools are applied systematically across the whole process. This approach suffers from taking a longer time to produce results but it is more engaging of the whole workforce. The longer time period can mean that managers give up before the change becomes embedded.

> **Beware!**
> Consultants almost always use only a pillar approach, which may not be best for you. Confronted with such advice, ask yourself: "Why am I being told this?"

We believe that sustainable change requires a judicious combination of both approaches, possibly starting with pillars, to act as pilots to test the tools and demonstrate their value, followed by a platform approach to roll them out across the plant.

Let us now continue our story by first looking at some of the Lean tools, technologies, and techniques that are often considered the foundations of a Lean enterprise and essential to managing such an enterprise. These tools are applicable across the whole organization, regardless of whether this is a manufacturing or service industry.

Lean Tools for *Managing* Lean Enterprises

Fundamental to Lean are the tools and techniques for empowering and involving employees and managing the Lean enterprise. At the heart of these are policy deployment, which we discussed in Chapter 3 on strategy and alignment, 5S, visual management, and problem solving. These tools are applicable everywhere in the organization, from the shop floor, through the commercial office environment, to the boardroom. We even saw examples of 5S in the washrooms at Cogent Power in Canada. Let us examine these in a little more detail.

5S: Workplace Organization

5S is a powerful system of workplace organization named after five Japanese terms translated as sort, set in order, shine, standardize, and sustain. At its basic level, it is good housekeeping; at another level, it is the first step in improving productivity. 5S is part of a visual workplace (Figure 7.3).

> 5S has made a huge difference in our area. It is tremendously better now; so much more organized than it used to be. You are not digging around trying to find things all the time.
> —Maintenance Leader, Cogent Power, Canada

We all feel better when we can find things easily, when they are clean and well maintained. We are more productive when we are not spending time looking for

Figure 7.3   5S – Workplace organization.

items, only to discover that when we find them, they are not fit for purpose. Even so, 5S does more than simply ensure that a workplace is tidy and well organized. 5S is a management tool that involves and empowers people, with five traditional steps:

1. *Sort*. As managers, you are saying to employees, "You decide what is necessary to do the job and sort out what you do and what you do not need." In this you are empowering people by giving them choice and responsibility to make decisions about their workstation.

2. *Set in order*. This requires management intervention to provide the means for appropriate storage: shadow boards, bins, trolleys, tool cabinets, etc. This demonstrates management commitment and involvement.

3. *Shine, sweep, or scrub* means taking responsibility for the cleanliness of the workstation; it also requires that management acknowledge that time for cleaning is part of the workday. In this step, a regime and standards for cleaning are made.

4. *Standardize* is about maintaining and supporting the first three steps; this requires employee buy-in and commitment. Standards on what things are kept (S1), where they are kept (S2), and by whom, with what, when, and how they are cleaned (S3) are made. At this stage, visual aids for 5S audits are created.

5. *Sustain*, or discipline; this is about making 5S a way of life and embedding it in the culture of the organization.

One of the primary reasons why 5S was sustainable at Cogent Power was that through their policy deployment approach, each employee understood why they were doing 5S and how it would help them achieve their own goals. In other words, it was a tool that was pulled by employees—it was not just another tool pushed at an unsuspecting workforce.

5S is often a platform approach starting a Lean implementation. It involves and empowers employees, and it has huge visual impact. It also releases capital and space held in holding obsolete stock and equipment. At Cogent Power, 5S was one of the first Lean tools implemented at all three plants. In Sweden it was highly influential. Carl, the Managing Director, found that it was a useful way of convincing people.

> The benefit with 5S is that it is very visual, involves everyone, and it can be easily accepted. 5S is an easy way to convince people.
> —Carl, Managing Director, Cogent Power, Sweden

Due to the consensus culture in Sweden, they took rather longer to start the implementation. Frans spent a lot of time helping Carl and Per, the Lean Manager, trying to convince the management team and unions of the benefits of Lean, and he built up considerable trust. Once they had started with 5S, they soon got employee buy-in and, when we met them, there was universal praise for the improvements that a clean and well-organized shop floor had delivered. As part of the exercise, they identified all the obsolete machinery and sold or removed it. This created space that was used to lay out maintenance areas better. These were cleaned, painted, and supplied with better lighting to make a cleaner, safer environment in which to work. All the tools were displayed on shadow boards, and other items were labeled and stored in new cabinets. Even the bicycles used by plant engineers to get around the site were given designated bays so that they could be easily located.

> The job is more structured now—all the tools are in the right place; it is much more organized.
> —Operator 1, Cogent Power, Sweden

> It is cleaner and organized now; I am proud to show my friends where I work.
> —Operator 2, Cogent Power, Sweden

Visual management and 5S are closely integrated. 5S maintains workplace organization by visual means, such as shadow boards and labeled containers. We now look at some other examples of visual management.

Visual Management

In Chapter 3 on *strategy and alignment*, we discussed A3 planning and business cockpits. These are forms of visual management aimed at making information available at the point of operation. The information presented should be timely and understandable to help everyone manage and improve the process. The visual management triangle (Figure 7.4) is based on the concept of shared knowledge and responsibility. If information is visible in the workplace, problems are detected earlier and improvements can be made, or monitored, more easily. Compare this to information held in a computer and accessible only to those people who have access to

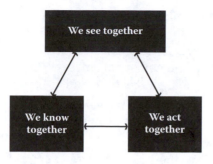

Figure 7.4   Visual Management triangle. (*Source:* Pascal Dennis, *Andy & Me: Crisis and Transformation on the Lean Journey*, Productivity Press, 2005.)

the computer screen. Visual management is much more immediate if it is available to groups of people who can share the knowledge and participate in problem solving. Typical information that you would expect to see in a Lean organization includes performance charts, skills matrices, schedules, team attendance, and health and safety records. One of the tests of Lean is seeing if information is visible and up to date.

Let us consider the Lean metrics here. You can use Table 7.2 to check the metrics in your own organization, but remember that the metrics should be easy to collect and understand. Also, they should be critically aligned to your customer, business, and employee needs. Making them too complex or difficult to collect is a waste. Record only the metrics that you need to manage and monitor the process efficiently and effectively.

Availability of the plant was a big issue at Cogent Power in Canada. Here they use OEE combined with other measures as their standard for performance. Production boards are displayed prominently on the shop floor. On

Table 7.2   Some typical Lean metrics.

Metric	Description	Used for:
Inventory Turns (Stock turns)	The number of times that an organization's inventory cycles or turns over per year.	Monitoring holding cost. Reducing holding costs improve profitability, as long as revenue from sales is constant.
Finished Goods Inventory	Number of units or days of finished goods stock.	Inventory management
Total Work In Process (WIP)	The number of units or days of work in progress.	Inventory management
Total Lead Time	The total time needed for an order to be processed.	Monitoring efficiency or lead-time
Total Cycle Time	Total time taken from start to end of a process.	Monitoring efficiency
On-Time Delivery In Full (OTIF)	On-Time Delivery In Full. The number of deliveries in a cycle that were delivered on-time and in full.	Monitoring delivery performance
Schedule Adherence	Internal measure of ability to hit target for quality and quantity on a day-by-day, line-by-line.	Monitoring internal consistency
Overall Equipment Effectiveness (OEE)	OEE is a measure of relative availability, performance and quality of plant or equipment. OEE% = Availability% × performance% × Quality%	Monitoring how well equipment is running compared to the ideal plant. Important for managing bottleneck equipment.

Table 7.2 Some typical Lean metrics. (Continued)

Metric	Description	Used for:
Right First Time (RFT)	Right First Time. The number of parts that are passed on free of defects compared with the total number of parts produced.	Monitoring quality
Lost-time Incidents	Number of accidents or other incidents that result in an employee losing time.	Monitoring health and safety
Attendance	Percentage of time that employees attended work. The reverse of absence, hence a positive measure.	Monitoring morale
Appropriate Skills	The percentage of skills types in each work area that have an appropriate level of cover.	Monitoring alignment and morale

each of these, the KPIs are color coded in each of the key areas: financial, customer satisfaction, employee well-being, and sustainability. Initially, the operators used to write the scores on pieces of paper and these were later entered into an IT system that calculated the values. In 2007 they changed to simpler calculations and made the team leader in each area responsible for entering the figures on a whiteboard. They employed a lot of psychology in this and it took four to five months to complete. There is a barrier to writing down your figures and displaying them if they are below target. It makes your personal or team performance visible.

Table 7.3 provides a typical chart. The color coding is standard across the plant, although the individual measures may change to be appropriate to a team or department. Where the trends are negative, they become a target for improvement. Improvement targets follow a standard procedure where problem-solving skills are used to define the problem and suggest countermeasures.

Table 7.3   Typical Cogent Power metrics chart.

Last Year	Description	This Month	KPI Target	Trend
	Financial			
27%	OEE	31%	35%	+ve
18	Inventory Turns	22	24	+ve
95%	Quality	90%	98%	-ve
	Customer Satisfaction			
93.1%	OTIF(External customer)	91%	100%	-ve
98.1%	OTIF (Internal customer)	99.3%	100%	+ve
4824	Customer Failure Rate (ppm)	6204	500	-ve
	Employee Well-being			
97%	Employee Attendance	98.1%	100%	+ve
0	LTA	0	0	+ve
	Sustainability			
46%	Process Audit/ 5S Scores	62%	85%	+ve
99.3%	Inventory Accuracy	99.5%	100%	+ve

Responsibility for the action is then given to the team, which sets up an improvement project. Note that it is the team that takes responsibility. If the actions are aligned as we discussed in Chapter 3 on strategy and alignment, then the team-level PDCA cycles drive the departmental projects, which drive the business level cycles—like a series of gears (Figure 7.5). The business cockpits are used to monitor these and make visible all the projects at each level. The effectiveness of the system as a whole is determined by the effectiveness of each zone: teams, groups, departments, and so on.

By putting the figures in public view, the team leaders are taking responsibility for the results. So the team leaders must be persuaded that, by highlighting the problems, they will be given the resources and help to improve. At Cogent Power in Canada, they are convinced that they would not have generated the improvements they saw if they had not made this change.

> This year we set a goal for ourselves in a major improvement in OEE and to do this we had to open the dam on spending on maintenance. We upgraded our maintenance crew and spent an

Figure 7.5　Continuous improvement gears.

ocean of money. I said to the two production managers that I would continue to allow an open spend on maintenance as long as OEE improved at an appropriate rate because that's the end result that we're looking for.

—Ron, Operations Director, Canada

Continuous improvement is keeping the gears turning and solving the problems that each project uncovers. Problem solving is like peeling an onion: each layer removed uncovers more layers. Common problem-solving tools include the 5 Whys. If you ask "why?" five times, you get closer to the real problem. Cogent Power uses 5 Whys and 4M fishbone diagrams to brainstorm the cause of problems. 4M refers to problems that derive from Man, Machine, Material, or Method issues. When the teams have defined the problems, they create continuous improvement projects to solve them. Mark, the General Manager at Cogent Power in the United Kingdom, was inspired by a quote from James Dyson, founder of Dyson Ltd.:

There is no such thing as a quantum leap. There is only dogged persistence and, in the end, you make it look like a quantum leap.

Based on this, Mark started a "Quantum Leap" initiative at Cogent Power, United Kingdom. In one brainstorming session, hundreds of actions were generated. As part of this, a new concept called "100 Day Projects" was introduced. Each action, or improvement project, must be completed in 100 days. The clock starts ticking as soon as the project starts, and the timeline is monitored by the leader at each zone. The team leader is monitored by his or her manager and then by the senior management team. The concept breaks down the problem into achievable steps, keeping the improvement moving forward and sustaining the culture of continuous improvement. This approach has also shown improvements in the involvement and engagement of employees. Employee suggestions are monitored as a measure of employee buy-in. In the first year, the suggestion scheme generated twenty-six suggestions; this had risen to fifty-four in the second year. And in the third year, when they embarked on Quantum Leap, this increased to 254; with 50 percent of suggestions being safety related and the other 50 percent process related. The proceeds of the improvements are put back into the business to improve the working environment, making the improvements both highly visible and engaging.

> The 100 day projects have been a remarkable success. We have seen benefits in the team dynamics and we have improved yield by reducing defects from 6,000 ppm to 500 ppm. We even installed a new quality system in 100 days.
> —Mark, General Manager, Cogent Power,
> United Kingdom

5S and Visual Management are tools that extend across the entire business. While all three plants have implemented these, in Sweden the main focus of Lean has been in 5S and Visual Management.

Lean Tools for *Operating* a Lean Enterprise

Lean operating systems are those that are designed on the five Lean principles: Understanding *value* from the customers' perspective, identify the *value stream*, make the value *flow*, at the *pull* of the customer, and strive for *perfection*.

The key to operating a Lean environment is making products and services that customers value flow at the same rate as the demand of the customer. In this section we look at how other Cogent Power plants have implemented Lean tools to improve flow.

The first step in creating flow is defining the customer demand; this is often done by defining the *takt* time, the rhythm or drumbeat of customer demand. The second step is to establish the capacity of the system and identify bottlenecks or constraints. As discussed previously when we looked at the order creation process, you cannot improve the process unless you understand it. Until you understand the capacity, you do not know where to target the improvements. If you apply Lean tools before you understand the process, you risk implementing inappropriate solutions. Take manufacturing to the takt time, for example. This could ensure that production matches the actual demand of the customer. However, when the process involves large pieces of a kit, such as ovens or smelters, it is not always practical to use takt time as the production rate. In this instance, kanbans, or time-based buffer stocks, should be used to control the flow through the bottleneck.

At Cogent Power in Canada, they have put in a pull system to manage the upstream processes but the oven remains a bottleneck. They manage the flow of these with buffers. For further information on managing bottlenecks and flow, see *The Goal* by Goldratt and Cox.

Some of the tools used to improve flow include

- Mapping to understand the flow and illustrate waste and blockages
- Standardized work to stabilize the process
- TPM and SMED to improve the reliability and reduce changeover and setup time

Cogent Power has used all these tools to improve the flow of materials.

Mapping

Physical products, information, and creative ideas all need to be allowed to flow through the value chain with minimum disruption and diversion. The first step in understanding the flow is *mapping* the processes.

The mapping process always starts with a review to test that the strategic objectives have been clearly defined and deployed; this is followed by a very detailed scoping and planning session. Once this is complete, the detailed mapping process and analysis can begin. We described big-picture value stream mapping and four fields mapping in the section on processes where they are used extensively in Cogent Power to map the order fulfillment and order creation processes. There are various additional mapping tools that can be used in a Lean environment. These include

- Process activity mapping
- Supply chain responsiveness
- Product variety funnel

- Quality filter mapping
- Decision point analysis
- Forrester effect (bullwhip) mapping
- Overall structure mapping

These tools were first described as the Seven Value Stream Mapping tools by Hines and Rich in *Value Stream Management* and are discussed in detail in *Lean Evolution: Lessons from the Workplace* by Rich et al. Figure 7.6 which includes Four Fields Mapping and another tool named Process Decomposition, shows which tool should be chosen to detect any particular form of waste. Using a combination of the appropriate mapping tools helps to better understand the business, and its issues, before designing a Lean improvement program.

Whichever mapping tool is selected, the process of mapping always starts with mapping the current state and, to be effective, should always be followed by a root cause analysis of the issues and concerns. The root cause analysis examines process and cultural issues and suggests possible solutions. Finally, the mapping exercise results in a future state map that is used as the basis to improve the flow of the process.

Cogent Power use the term "line of sight" to make sure that the future state map and the improvement opportunities identified by the mapping are aligned to the strategy.

> Cogent's line of sight processes (LOS) are an integral part of mapping out the future within our company; identifying our plans, visions and goals; and communicating how we are doing against our desired results.

Need	Tools								
	Product Family Analysis	Process Decomposition	Big Picture Mapping	Process Activity Map	Four Fields Map	Supply Chain Response Matrix	Product Variety Funnel	Quality Filter Map	Demand Amplification Map
Gain an overview	●	●	●			●			
Decide where to start	●	●							
Scope a process		●	●		●				
Working with physical products	●		●	●		●	●	●	●
Working with information	●		●		●				
Getting into fine detail				●	●		●	●	●
Working across organizations			●			●			

Figure 7.6 Value stream mapping tools. (Adapted from Peter Hines and Nick Rich, *The seven value stream mapping tools*, 1997.)

The term "line of sight" specifically refers to the alignment created through our communication and information-sharing processes that permit everyone to see how the work that they do each day, and how the work and results that they achieve, are linked specifically to the goals, vision, and desired performance results of the company. This helps

■ Know what desired results exist, for the company and its work area
■ Know what the current status is, and what plans and actions are in place to improve the results
■ Know how we are performing with key customer measures—like OTIF, product and service nonconformances, and other value added performance factors; and the waste reduction work and results.

Line-of-sight huddles will be an integral part of our LOS process, as a means of active communication of our important work and team engagement.
—*Thinking Lean: Putting It All Together*, Cogent Lean Management System booklet, Ron and Greg, Cogent Power, Canada

Standardized Work

At Toyota, work is broken down into operations. Each operation is standardized so that everyone performs the same actions to do the same work, whether this is operating or maintaining a machine or running a project. By continually performing activities in the same way, they become routine and embedded as the "way of life." Standard methods make sustaining the Lean transformation and continual improvement easier. If everyone behaves differently each time they perform a task, it is more difficult to make improvements, and easier to revert to old habits. Standardized work methods improve performance because tasks can be taught to new employees more easily and processes are easier to audit. Having standards makes abnormalities more visible and persistent problems more repeatable; this makes problem solving more straightforward. In *Creating a Lean Culture: Tools to Sustain Lean Conversions*, Mann discusses standard work for leaders as one of the principal elements of a Lean management system.

> Standardized work conditions create an environment where each team member in a process is working effectively and safely, able to repeat a sequence of steps in a consistent manner that produces the highest quality of product, with the least possible waste. At Cogent we call these "Safe Work Standards."
> —*Thinking Lean: Putting It All Together*, Cogent Lean Management System booklet, Ron and Greg, Cogent Power, Canada

Cogent Power in Canada has recently started the conversion of standard operating procedures to a format called job instructions (JI), based on training within industry (TWI). There are two important aspects to JI:

1. The procedural systems are documented in a manner that makes them simple, easy to follow, with the necessary steps in a process clearly defined; and
2. The training method used with the JI is a superior process to what typically is used in manufacturing training.

The JI training method requires leaders and operating team members to work through the detailed aspects of the process steps until there is a clear and demonstrated understanding of the steps to the work. A follow-up audit component of this training ensures that processes are current and being followed, and a consistency of practice is created. Together, the Safe Work Standard and JI are key to Cogent Power's ability to generate world-class improvements.

Once the processes have been mapped and the standard operations defined, it is time to look at the reliability of the plant and the equipment that supports the ability to flow.

One of the TPS pillars is just in time (JIT). To operate JIT requires that the machines are reliable and available, operators are skilled and capable, and demand from customers can be translated to signals on the shop floor and to the material suppliers. This involves total productive maintenance (TPM) to improve machine reliability, training and development programs to ensure operator skills, and pull signals from customer demand.

Total Productive Maintenance

TPM is a technique designed to optimize the performance, reliability, and productivity of plant and equipment. It involves passing the responsibility for maintenance into the hands of the operators and seeks to address the "six big losses" that affect equipment performance and reliability. TPM links directly to OEE as the six big losses are divided into three categories: availability, performance, and quality (Figure 7.7).

Figure 7.7 Overall equipment effectiveness (OEE) = Availability x Performance x Quality.

These categories are the basis of OEE. People often think that TPM refers only to manufacturing or production, but the term is Total *Productive* Maintenance, and the concept applies as much to the office environment as it does to the shop floor. Think for a moment in terms of computer hardware and networks as equipment. Computers and networks break down, causing availability issues. Networks run slowly, affecting performance. Incomplete or erroneous data causes rejects and rework, quality issues.

Beware!
OEE can drive the wrong behaviors as OEE can be shown to go up by increasing batch size and reducing changeovers. We saw another company that proudly displayed their "world-class" doubling of OEE to 85 percent... but at the cost of a trebling (overproducing) finished stock. So make sure that OEE calculations are always combined with other measures, such as stock turns and schedule adherence.

Availability

Breakdown losses due to equipment failure are unplanned stoppages that require repair. These are usually counted as a breakdown if the stops are longer than ten minutes. It is important to record the *nature* and *cause* of the stoppage, whether it is electrical, mechanical, hydraulic, or pneumatic. Improvement is about eliminating the cause of breakdown.

Changeover includes set-up and run-up adjustment losses that occur when one product is changed to another. Changeover is measured by the time it takes between the normal operating speeds of one product to the normal operating speed of another. SMED (Single-Minute Exchange of Die) is the objective for fast changeover, where equipment can be changed from one product to the next in less than ten minutes. SMED is integral to TPM. We will come back to SMED later.

Performance

Idling and minor stoppages are those that are less than ten minutes. The causes of these are many and may include jams, material loading, removal of debris, and small adjustments. In an analysis, it is often found that minor stoppages create the most downtime. It is important to record the number of minor stoppages as these are often ignored.

Reduced speed losses result from running the machine more slowly than the design speed due to problems with materials, worn tools or belts, and other causes. This can be calculated by recording the actual production and then comparing this to the expected production for a given time period.

Quality

Process defects that result in scrap or rework are usually the result of problems that cause the machine to work outside of its specification.

Reduced yield may be a result of poor materials but can also result from material losses during changeover when old material is running out and new material is running in.

TPM is essential in a Lean environment as equipment reliability is a critical component. Equipment reliability directly influences inventory levels, as stock levels would have to be increased to cover breakdowns, poor quality, and lost time. So, improving reliability through a TPM program can improve OEE and allow you to reduce inventory. Rich discusses TPM in detail in *Total Productive Maintenance: The Lean Approach*.

Cogent Power used a TPM process model that started with collecting OEE data and managing by fact. 5S was used to organize the workplace and design the workstation so that the tools and spares necessary for maintaining the equipment were labeled, available, and replenished when required.

TPM projects involved multidisciplinary teams of operators and engineers with agreed roles and responsibilities and defined skills training. Project teams worked simultaneously on the two outside pillars to stabilize the equipment condition and improve the man-machine interface. As each project neared completion, support systems and methods to sustain the improvement capability were established. The improvements included visibly marking all gauges and lubrication points, having tools and spares located at point of use, and setting standards to ensure that the process was easy to operate, maintain, clean, check, set up, and change over. As a result of TPM activities, OEE improved significantly at all three Cogent Power plants.

Let us now return to SMED to discuss how they reduced the changeover and set-up time in Canada.

Single-Minute Exchange of Die (SMED)

Changeovers are part of OEE and thus SMED activities are included as part of a TPM program. Initially, the place to concentrate on SMED is at the bottleneck resources. There is little point in reducing set-ups on non-bottlenecks until you have first focused on and improved the machines that are actually constraining flow.

When implementing SMED activities, Cogent Power followed a four-phase analysis process using the classic Shigeo Shingo methods.

The process started by forming a multidisciplinary team, including operators, engineers, and planners. Taking a PDCA approach, team members collected data on demand, machine performance, OEE trends, and sequence dependencies. They videotaped and timed the current state and used the videotapes to separate "internal" from "external" activities. They mapped the current state against a timeline on large sheets of brown paper and used these to identify opportunities for improvement. SMED projects included 5S on the changeover tools and dies, changing layouts, simplifying and resequencing some activities, as well as making any necessary engineering changes. *Poka-yoke* (or mistake proofing) devices and visual controls were established.

Targets for improvement were fixed and priorities were established. A paper kaizen of the future state was developed to model the improved changeover. The activities were planned and implemented in a phased process, each phase followed by checking and adjusting in classic PDCA style. When the new process was finally established, standard operating procedures (SOPs) were developed and operators trained. Remember, however, that once the SOPs are created, they must be maintained and audited to sustain the improvement.

SOPs in a Lean enterprise are dynamic and set by operators consensually. They should be written by the operators in their own words and adapted with continual improvement. They should not be rigidly scripted; rather, they should be flexible and adaptable, and should include detailed work sequences, timing, and any standard inventory or kanban requirements. Good SOPs make use of photographs that show normal conditions and settings. They should also contain instructions on what to do if something goes wrong. Finally, they should be visible: positioned on the machine at the point of use.

TPM and SMED have been implemented in all three Cogent Power plants; it has been a particular focus in the United Kingdom and Canada sites. In the next section we look at some of the tools and techniques used to operate the just-in-time (JIT) pillar of Lean enterprises and illustrate these with examples from Cogent Power.

Just-in-Time (JIT)

> We manufacture products based on customer orders. We keep a minimum of inventory so that we can provide our customers with the materials that they need, without the wastes associated with stockpiles of material and finished goods. Our processes need to focus on providing continuously shorter lead times to allow customers to manufacture only on the basis of their customer needs, not on forecasts. This creates activities based on the pull of the customer, and a continuous flow of goods.
>
> —*Thinking Lean: Putting It All Together*, Cogent Lean Management System booklet, Ron and Greg, Cogent Power, Canada

Pull Systems

Pull signals are based on response to actual customer demand, not in response to orders *pushed* onto the shop floor from schedules based on forecasts. Pull is based on a sell-one (or use-one), make-one concept. We believe that implementing pull systems should come later in a Lean transition, as it is not something that can be sustainably embarked upon until the system is stable and capable. For example, demand needs to be as smooth as possible to eliminate spikes and allow the products to flow. Think for a moment about where pull comes into the five Lean principles. It comes fourth, just before striving for perfection.

Let us just remind ourselves of the five Lean principles (Figure 7.8) to see what must be in place before we can implement pull.

First we need to know what customers value. We need to have identified the value stream and been able

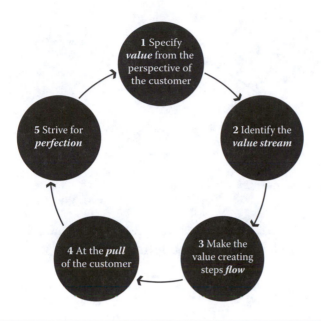

Figure 7.8   Five Lean Principles. (*Source:* Adapted from Jim Womack and Dan Jones, *Lean Thinking: Banish Waste and Create Wealth in your Corporation*, 1996.)

to make value-creating steps flow and then we can pull products to customer demand. Pull systems need to be aligned with strategy, supported by senior management and operated by skilled employees (Figure 7.9).

Pull may not be the best strategy for all products; some products (strangers) that are made infrequently may be best left to be "made to stock" and replenished when needed. One of the techniques for selecting which products to put onto a pull system is to use the "runners, repeaters, and strangers" concept.

- *Runners* are products, or product families, that have sufficient volume to be produced very frequently, typically every day. They are usually high volume, low variability. Sometimes these products justify dedicated lines.

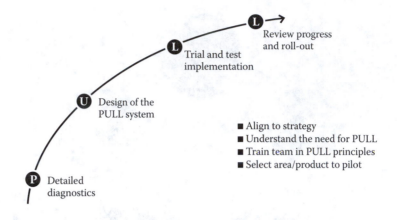

Figure 7.9 Pull system implementation.

- *Repeaters* are products, or product families, with intermediate volume and variety that are made frequently but not necessarily every day, and the volumes do not justify dedicated lines.
- *Strangers* are products, or product families, that are made infrequently and are often highly variable.

> Beware of simplistic Lean texts that assume everything you make is a runner product … you will end up putting in kanban systems everywhere. If you have stranger or even repeater products, you will be creating a sustainability disaster!

A Pareto analysis (80/20) can be used to categorize products into runner, repeaters, and strangers. Pull systems are best suited for runners and some repeaters with short lead-times. Strangers are not likely candidates for pull systems. However, it should always be the aim to convert repeaters to runners and strangers to repeaters.

The concept of a pull system can be applied to both information flows as well as materials flows to avoid batching paper or information steps in a process. Integral to pull systems is responding to a signal that represents customer demand. One of the ways of signaling production in a pull system is by *kanbans*. This is the system they have adopted in the Cogent Power Canada plant.

Kanbans

Kanbans are signaling systems that are the means through which JIT is achieved. The term "kanban" derives from *kan*, meaning visual, and *ban*, meaning card or board. Traditionally, kanbans were developed as two-card systems, although now there are many other forms, including squares, balls, and lights.

The principle behind kanban is that products are only made, or moved, when a signal is given. In a card system, there is traditionally a withdrawal card and a production ordering card: that is, a *make* card. Take the example in Figure 7.10 from Monden's book entitled *Toyota Production System*. An assembly line is making products A, B, and C in sequence. The parts used in production are a, b, and c, which are being machined by an upstream process. Parts a, b, and c each have a *make* card attached to them. The material handler from the assembly line will go to the store with a *withdrawal* card for part a. When the part is withdrawn from the store, the *make* card is taken off and sent back to the machine line to produce another part a. The number of kanbans in the system is determined by customer demand. The kanban system is supported by leveled scheduling, SMED, standardized operations, and Jidoka.

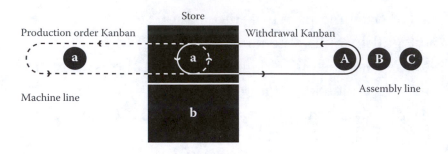

Figure 7.10 The flow of two Kanbans. (*Source:* Adapted from Yasuhiro Monden, *Toyota Production System*, 1988.)

Kanbans help reduce inventory and eliminate over-production. They can easily be extended to the supply chain by sending the *make* signal (physically or electronically) to the downstream suppliers. Kanbans can also be used in the visual office environment—for example, replenishing printer paper. If the boxes of paper have an indicator card to show when more must be collected or produced, then there is less chance of running out and disrupting the workflow. We probably all use mental kanbans at home, in our kitchens, bathrooms, or garages. After all, what is an empty toilet paper roll holder, if not a kanban signal?

At Cogent Power, they make good use of kanbans to manage supplies. They use kanban boards to manage internal stocks, have developed an innovative way of using technology to manage material stocks from their suppliers, and are extending it to their customers to help manage finished goods stocks. At the Canadian plant, they have installed Web cameras that are directed at pallet locations. The suppliers that are responsible for the supplies to these pallet locations are connected to the cameras and they can check the status of the stocks. The stocks are marked by red, amber, and green levels; when the stock reaches an amber level, this is the signal to prepare to produce and ship more products to replenish the stock to the green level. If stock hits the red level, the supplier must have the stock due for delivery, or must have notified the plant of a delivery date. The term they have used for this is "cambans."

Cambans are now installed in the finished goods area. These are connected to key customers who can check the finished goods stock that is being held for them by Cogent Power as part of a vendor-managed inventory (VMI) system. The customers can use the information to improve their forward planning and to inform Cogent Power of any changes to their demand profiles.

We have discussed the TPS pillar of JIT but we need to remember that TPS has two pillars: JIT and Jidoka.

Jidoka

Jidoka refers to the practice of immediately stopping work or work processes to address a failure or a problem with product or information quality. The Jidoka process is designed to make problems visible and to give authority to everyone to immediately stop work to solve problems.

This process is ideally suited to production operation processes, as machinery or materials often contribute to failures to achieve desired product quality. Immediately upon identifying a failure in product quality, the production operator or team stops work and solves the problem.

This problem may require additional resources as identified by the operating team and its leaders. Cogent Power uses indicating lights, often called *andon* lights, to identify when a production stop has occurred, and the needed resources are being applied to correct the situation. The team then goes through the Jidoka problem-solving process to identify and correct the root causes of the problem, thereby eliminating the wastes associated with continuing production without a resolution.

The problem-solving process used at Cogent Power is based on the A3 process, a problem-solving tool developed and used for many years within the TPS. It uses an A3 report as part of a formalized problem-solving process, and is so named because it is written on A3-sized paper (metric equivalent of 11 by 17 inches).

The template for Cogent Power's version of the A3 problem-solving report covers key aspects in the problem-solving process:

■ Background and current conditions of the problem
■ Definition of the desired results
■ Problem analysis and cause study
■ Outline countermeasures needed to improve the results
■ Definition of the plan for improvement
■ A follow-up process to ensure that desired results are being achieved

Cogent Power considers that a formal problem-solving process is needed within their business to tackle more complicated issues and problems in a formalized and visual way.

Solving problems is a key aspect of continuous improvement and our accountability model. The A3 process also reinforces the plan-do-check-act (PDCA) circular model of continuous improvement. The A3 process is applied equally as a problem-solving tool to errors in information flow, such as production scheduling, work orders, product identification, or specifications.

We have considered the tools and techniques for managing and operating Lean environments. Let us now turn attention to some of those that can be used to *sustain* a Lean environment.

Tools and Techniques to *Sustain* a Lean Environment

When asked what makes a Lean change stick, many managers have told us that it is leaders who "walk the talk" and implement effective measures and monitoring systems. At Cogent Power, Marcel and Frans were adamant that leaders at all levels embrace the change and lead the Lean lifestyle.

> Lean is not a one-off event that you can measure by a return on income. Lean is a lifestyle and a way of running your business.
> —Bill, Director, Electrical Steels, United Kingdom and Sweden

Leading the Lean lifestyle was the focus at Cogent Power in the United Kingdom. Marcel and Frans were often found on the shop floor or in offices, and they expected to see Lean being practiced wherever they went. The emphasis here has been on sustainability of the whole rather than the application of individual tools and techniques. They took a "one step at a time" approach, applying tools and techniques to deliver quick wins that could be used to demonstrate the benefits of leading the Lean lifestyle. Once the message had gotten across, they progressed to more ambitious, long-range projects. Of particular importance here has been visual management, through the cockpits and regular process auditing.

Sustainability Audits

Audits are a way of life in a Cogent Power plant. There are weekly audits of 5S and equipment conditions. These are displayed prominently and discussed at management meetings. Actions that occur as a result of the audit are given to teams to resolve, such as "red tag" issues. Red tags are put on equipment that requires attention. The outstanding issues and the team responsible are displayed, and the status of the action is recorded. At Cogent Power, they have defined a standard for plant and process audit criteria (Figure 7.11) that everyone follows.

As previously discussed, the pace of change at each Cogent plant was different.

As well as internal audits, the Lean implementation itself is audited. The audit is conducted by external auditors and is designed to measure Lean maturity and sustainability.

The method of establishing the level of Lean maturity was developed by S A Partners and looks not only at *what* is being done, but more importantly at *how* it is being

Figure 7.11 Cogent Power plant and process audit criteria.

done. In other words, the sustainability audit measures not just what the company does, but also—and more importantly—the *way* in which it does it. This helps to build a learning organization that not only has the capability to maintain the gains of the improvement, but also an organization that is self-propelled continuously to improve the continuous improvement process until it becomes a daily habit for everyone.

The sustainability audit quantifiably and subjectively measures the maturity of both process and behaviors in all aspects of business: strategy alignment, leadership, engagement, process and supply-chain management, and the application of Lean tools. This provides a balanced approach to their Lean initiatives and acts as a guide for the basic business elements that must be addressed throughout their Lean journey. The scoring index for maturity starts at level 1, where an organization takes an ad hoc or reactive approach to improvement (Figure 7.12). The maturity then moves through the milestones of formal, goal-oriented, managed autonomy and finally on to level 5, where Lean has become the way of life and the entire organization is capable of self-sustaining continuous improvement.

Using this diagnosis, in line with the future state vision for Lean Maturity and the business strategy, it provides the appropriate context to create a road map (Figure 7.13) for how to progress from the current state to the future state.

By understanding the current reality of every aspect of the business model and articulating what you want to achieve (i.e., what will good look like and what will be the tangible benefits to the business), you will be

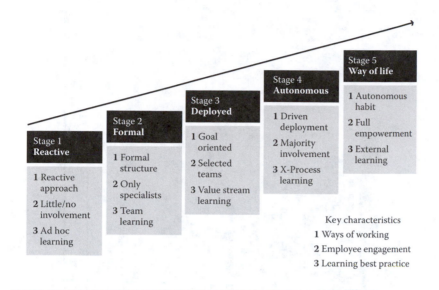

Figure 7.12   The milestones of Lean maturity.

able to develop a top-level business road map. At a high level, the road map identifies which element you should place early emphasis on and which element requires later emphasis. As such, the model starts not only to provide a blueprint, but the assessment also leads to a road map for becoming Lean.

This audit process helped to identify the early weaknesses in the Lean implementation at Cogent Power. It also confirmed that organizational learning was taking place. As the organization learned, it was able to develop more sophisticated approaches that took the company to a new level. Opportunities that were not possible or could not have been imagined at the beginning emerged and took shape. Individuals began to make more challenging suggestions that took them and their teams out of their comfort zones. People started asking when improvements were going to be made in their areas and expectations rose.

Lean business model factor	2007 (focus for Improvement)	PDCA	2009 (future vision)
Strategy and alignment	Further simplify and reduce the KPIs to the Vital Few and encourage a 'bias for action' at all levels	→	Everybody understands their contribution to achieving strategy through deployment of a simple set of KPIs
Process management	Refine the strategic growth policy and co-ordinate improvements for an integrated set of commercial processes	→	Robust processes for order creation, innovation and new product introduction exist to support a clear growth strategy
People enabling processes	Provide the appropriate development for middle and line managers to enable their effective support and coordination of Continuous Improvement	→	Line level managers throughout the organization are capable of, and motivated to, autonomously support Continuous Improvement
Lean tools	Enhance approach to best practice sharing and learning to help accelerate and sustain balanced Continuous Improvement	→	The process of sharing best practice is a daily habit that encourages innovation within the bounds of the Cogent Way
Supply chain integration	Initiate and drive strategic cross-divisional steel supply chain improvement program	→	A mutually beneficial supply chain strategy is in place with our supply chain partners and 100% OTIF is achieved

Figure 7.13 Audit results road map 2007.

In 2007, Greg, the Lean Manager at Cogent Power, Canada, told us that he thinks that they have got Lean now. Instead of him and the Lean coaches *pushing* Lean at every opportunity and sending people on training courses, they are now *pulling* Lean. People are now asking, "Is this Lean?" every time they do something new and are challenging established ways of doing everything. As a result, they have adopted Lean and continuous improvement as the Cogent way of life.

A Word About the Technologies

Many early Lean practitioners held the view that IT was not necessary for Lean operations and considered that enterprise resource planning (ERP) systems were only suited for traditional "batch and queue," push scheduling environments.

Without a doubt, the concepts behind materials requirements planning (MRP), manufacturing resource planning (MRPII), and ERP were based on forecasts; from these, plans were generated and operations executed. It has long been recognized that forecasts are usually wrong, plans are too inflexible, and push concepts lead to overproduction and waste. However, the reality of managing the Lean demand-driven approach without the help of software is very difficult. In addition, many business measures that are essentially financial use data derived from the ERP system to monitor performance.

It is important to continually review the monitoring system during a Lean implementation, as many traditional cost accounting measures are inconsistent with pull systems and conflict can arise when performance measures have not been adapted in line with the new Lean processes.

An example here might be departmental productivity measures developed when departments had individual schedules and targets. These measures are no longer appropriate, or even collectable, in a Lean process-focused, cross-functional environment; and if departmental managers continue to be measured against inappropriate performance indicators, they will naturally regress to old methods so as to improve their "performance."

Instead of using MRP at the Canadian plant, Cogent Power developed a model for long-term planning that uses information generated from the ERP system to drive long-term purchase requirements.

> We don't use MRP anymore. MRP doesn't work very well with the long lead-times for steel and short order notice from our customers, but we do use our ERP system to manage our purchasing. We operate VMI that is handled by our ERP system. From the initial data entry, everything is handled electronically by barcodes. We have full traceability back to the mill with 98 percent data accuracy, so we only need to stock check biannually now.
> —Greg, Logistics and Purchasing Manager, Cogent Power, Canada

Critical to designing any production system, whether a manufacturing or service industry, is a clear understanding of the current capacity to meet customer demands and the ability to plan reliably for future growth. A capacity planning system is the key to this and is the first step in identifying bottlenecks in a process.

Imagine the following situation. You have attended the courses, read all the books, and designed your pull system. How did it work in reality? Often, the answer is "not very well"; things got out of sequence and the kanbans had to be overruled to meet deadlines. This has happened to us as well, so you are not alone.

What we found was that not all plants can work to takt time. Take, for example, large ovens, autoclaves, chemical baths, etc.; these are natural batch processes. And in a service environment too, it is not always possible to perform single-piece flow. Imagine in a busy office having to go to find someone to get them to sign off on the checks or purchase orders one at a time; the natural tendency would be to batch some jobs. Also, the best value stream mapping does not always spot the shared resources, those machines, tools, or labor that operate in multiple value streams; so things wait in queues. Generally when things wait in queues, someone will come along and reprioritize, usually to meet whoever is shouting loudest, or whatever returns the highest figures. Know the feeling?

When we were in this position, we realized that understanding the capacity is an essential step that you must take before you can design any flow system. Without knowing what your system is capable of, you cannot make decisions to flow products, services, or information.

Understanding the capacity of the system to meet current and future needs is an essential tool for operations managers. It is fundamental to facilities design, scheduling, and setting priorities for Lean improvements. Yet it is often surprising how little is known about the real capacity of a plant or business. There may be a number of the reasons for this; the operational system is very complex and often the measures are designed for financial planning rather than operational planning. Also, the internal machine environment may consist of a mix of natural batch resources as well as continuous processes and combining the machine, labor, and tooling constraints makes total capacity difficult to model.

Monitoring the capacity and work in progress (WIP) tells a lot about the internal operational system. To understand the system, you need to start by analyzing the operational capacities and WIP. In doing this, you identify the bottleneck constraints that disrupt the flow of goods or services. As Goldratt has pointed out, it is the constraints that determine the throughput. It is only with IT that you can do this effectively.

In a Lean implementation, once the value from the customer's perspective and the value streams have been identified, understanding the capacity to deliver is the next step in designing flow or pull systems.

There are many other examples of the use of technology at Cogent Power. They have used IT creatively to develop the cambans (described previously in their pull systems), and this is currently being extended across the supply chain to include vendor-managed inventory for key customers. In addition, at Cogent Power they are constantly striving to improve the information flow and reduce the need for manual rekeying of data. They have worked with customers and installed software, essentially an advanced print driver, which is linked to the Internet. When the customer prints a purchase order, it is transferred via the Web and input directly into the Cogent Power ERP system, thus saving substantial effort and time.

Maintaining misaligned legacy systems and redundant key business measures is wasteful and potentially damaging. It is very important to involve the finance and IT people early in a Lean transformation, as the IT systems and financial measures must be adapted to keep pace with the Lean change program. Where these cannot be modified, there should be no hesitation to replace them because they will severely limit the performance of improvements and this often makes Lean stall.

Where the IT systems and business measures are aligned, enhanced performance improvements can be expected and the change is more likely to stick. Aside from financial gains, benefits of aligned Lean and IT include enhanced visibility across the supply chain, increased flexibility and responsiveness, lead-time reduction, and increased productivity.

Summary

Technology, tools, and techniques: What we often find is

- Poor sustainability, especially of a Kaizen Blitz (only) approach
- Technology, tools, and techniques (TTT) used without understanding customer's needs
- TTT used without understanding business needs
- TTT thrown at problems, often in the wrong order
- People do not understand the quality side of Lean
- Used on shop floors only

■ A lot of wasted opportunities as people become "tool heads" without realizing that these are just tools (means/end reversion)

Applying Lean tools and techniques alone will not make an organization Lean. These are just things that Lean organizations use to help solve problems and support their Lean strategy. Ask yourself, "Is there any reason why a traditional mass producer cannot use 5S, Visual Management, TPM, and SMED?" No, there is no reason why they cannot use them, but without the Lean philosophy they will still be traditional mass producers. Real Lean organizations are not just companies that have successfully applied Lean tools; rather, they are organizations that have successfully adopted the Lean philosophy; they have a vision and a clear, aligned sense of *purpose*; and they have organized their business around key business *processes*. They have developed the right *people*, from the top to the bottom of the organization, who are engaged and exhibit the right behaviors, people who are capable of *"leading the Lean lifestyle."*

The TTT learning points can be summarized as follows:

■ Early application of the basic tools and techniques needs an emphasis on self-sustaining systems of management.
■ Lean tools and techniques are not an end in themselves. To achieve long-lasting results, they must be applied logically to solve defined problems rather than simply taking a scatter-gun approach.

- Use appropriate "bundles" and "combinations" of Lean tools and techniques to achieve specific value stream goals and financial improvements.
- Key value streams should be strategically selected and supported by senior management.
- KPIs should be simplified and monitored to ensure that they are appropriate and linked to the strategy.
- Use simple and proven technologies such as Web cams and software to better manage and make the bridge between customer and supplier demand profiles.
- Align Lean and IT to avoid waste and enhance the benefits.

Use our template (see Figure 8.13e) in Chapter 8 to assess how well your organization uses Lean tools, techniques, and technology.

IV
THE ROAD FROM PUSH TO PULL

The route through the "iceberg" is not always smooth, and which route a company takes depends on its organizational characteristics: the strategy, structure, culture, learning abilities, and goals, as well as the product/process mix, factory layout, and the age and condition of the plant and equipment.

Cogent Power's journey to Lean involved addressing all elements of the sustainable Lean Iceberg, but the progress they made reflected local decisions and corporate policies. A number of important lessons were learned as a result.

As we will see, the route that Cogent Power took reflected its immediate goals and stage of organizational learning.

Chapter 8

Route to Lean

Let us remind ourselves of the journey taken by Cogent Power as they traveled through their Lean transformation. Their journey started with Marcel announcing his vision to the senior managers. At that time it was understood that Cogent Power was in poor financial health, making huge losses, and a rapid turnaround was needed.

Although Marcel announced his intentions to the management team in December 2003, the transformation program was launched officially in January 2004 with the aim of stemming the financial losses and making the company more productive. Progress was reviewed formally in July 2005 and, despite making considerable advances, some concerns arose regarding the pace and sustainability of change. As a result, the road map of the journey changed slightly and more emphasis was put on what we now recognize as the "below the waterline" elements of a sustainable Lean Iceberg.

In this chapter we explore the road maps in more detail and illustrate the route they took by using circles and numbers to signify the stages. The size of each circle represents the emphasis that was placed, in terms of effort, on each of the elements.

The first phase of the transformation (see Figure 8.1) took approximately 18 months and resulted in establishing an awareness of Lean within the organization. The training and communication programs that were started in this phase involved many people, although they did not engage everyone totally in the transformation. There were still many skeptics and those who had "seen it all before."

The emphasis at this stage was on getting the right management team together and applying Lean tools and techniques to improve productivity. At this stage, it mainly focused on order fulfillment. This is illustrated by a fishbone diagram (Figure 8.2).

Although there was considerable improvement in productivity and also sound progress in the financial turnaround, the senior managers were concerned about both the pace and the scope of change; some sites and areas were seemingly progressing better than others. As

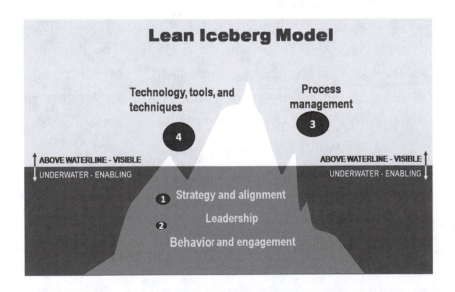

Figure 8.1   Roadmap 1 (2003–2005) of the Lean Iceberg Model.

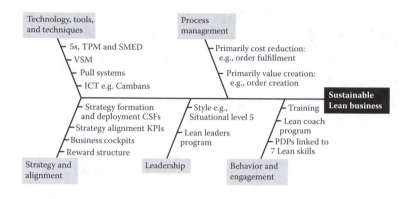

Figure 8.2 Fishbone analysis of roadmap 1.

a result, a Lean assessment was conducted and a number of issues were identified (Table 8.1).

There were also some other areas of concern:

■ Some people were still identified as "roadblocks" to progress, and a formal process of confronting these people was needed.

■ Organizational structures were still traditionally set by function and needed to be better aligned with value streams.

■ Establishing what "Best Practice" looks like for the business sector and setting new and improved standards for the Cogent Way would help visualize the goal for the operating units.

This is not unusual at this stage and it is often where many Lean implementations stagger or stall.

We describe the situation that we saw here as a narrowing of the iceberg beneath the waterline. It happens when the emphasis has been placed on the activities above the waterline: the processes, technology, tools,

Table 8.1   Issues raised by Lean assessment and key learnings in each theme.

Key Theme	Key Learning from Lean Experience
Leadership, Behavior and Engagement	The coaches who had been deployed to help drive the program had become the real leaders of Lean and it was accepted that, in taking a top-down and bottom-up approach to the program, the middle managers had been neglected. It was evident that they were not owning Lean and therefore not "Living the Lean Lifestyle" which is so critical to sustainability.
Strategy and Alignment	Although KPIs had been reasonably well deployed during the first round of deployment, a second round was needed to ensure that process teams and individuals were aligned with a full "line of sight" to the business strategy.
Process Management	In common with traditional businesses, customer value was perceived as merely quality, cost, and delivery (QCD), and the business had not yet really captured the true voice of the customer. It was also agreed that not enough effort had been given to applying Lean tools to help improve the way non-manufacturing process were managed.
Technology, Tools and Techniques	Key Value Streams needed to be strategically selected with more emphasis on "bottom-line" improvement activity. The Value Stream mapping improvements had been focused on building internal stability and it was recognized that, to make a real impact, work was needed across the extended enterprise. The use of technology to better manage end-to-end supply chain "Pull" systems would make a difference.

and techniques. In this case, because of the turnaround situation, this was the correct path, but only for a certain period. This is the time when companies think that they have implemented Lean. In reality, this is often when the implementation is in its most precarious and vulnerable state. To achieve sustainable results, the focus should be increasingly below the waterline, to build strong foundations and to support and keep the business afloat.

To Marcel, Frans, and Peter, it signaled a need to refocus and address the shortcomings (Figure 8.3).

A key part of this second phase was a focus on leadership, behavior, and engagement (Figure 8.4). There had been a lot of strategic Lean work at the senior management level and also Lean implementation at shop-floor level. However, this top-down meets bottom-up approach had left the middle community lacking the skill, competence, and motivation needed to take Lean to the next level. Extra training was put in at the middle management level so that the line managers and team leaders were given skills that emphasized the change in roles and responsibilities that were expected of the entire leadership community going forward, thereby helping individuals and teams to "lead the Lean lifestyle."

Another focus during the second phase was on the maturity with which the business units were able to apply "bundles" of tools and techniques in order to achieve real performance improvements. This came from enhanced, or "double-loop," learning, where the senior management teams of the plants began reviewing the profit potential of the various value streams and, based on volumes, margin, and future growth criteria, were

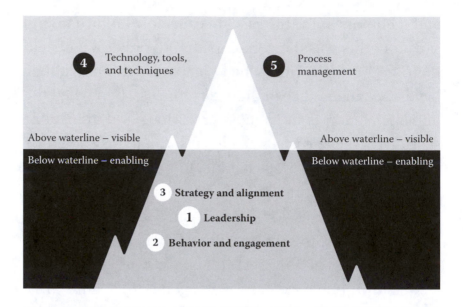

Figure 8.3   Roadmap 2 (2005–2007) on the Lean Iceberg model.

able to select, with knowledge, the key areas of focus for the operating teams to work on.

An integral part of the success was the recognition that the company needed to put into practice the first principle of Lean and better understand what its customers (both existing and new) really valued in a supplier. The organization needed to understand completely the true

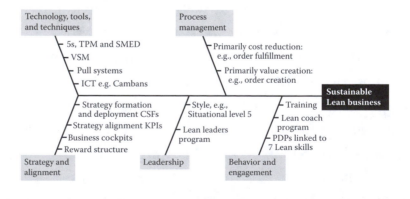

Figure 8.4   Fishbone analysis of roadmap 2.

"voice of the customer." Again, the timing was right here as by this stage the company was in a position to act on its understanding.

This is best illustrated by the following graphs developed by Mark and John from Cogent Power (United Kingdom) with help from the consultant, Gary, to show their progress in improving operational performance (efficiency) and commercial effectiveness in a changing market environment. Business Position 1 (Figure 8.5) was the starting point of the Lean transformation, with little focused effort on operational efficiency and weak commercial effectiveness.

Business Position 2 (Figure 8.6) was midway through the program. Operational efficiency had improved significantly but the external market had changed, making survival easier.

Business Position 3 (Figure 8.7) showed the improvement in commercial effectiveness but the strong market conditions were enhancing the overall business performance. The challenge now was to continue the improvements to be able to thrive, or survive, when the market for electrical steels returned to normal.

Lowering the Waterline: Rigorous, Not Glamorous

Since 2007 the market has changed and, although efficiency and effectiveness has improved, the thrive-survive boundary has shifted back to the configuration in Business Position 1, putting Business Position 4 back into the Survive zone. Back in 2003, Cogent Power had started at a place that was, for the industry, somewhat

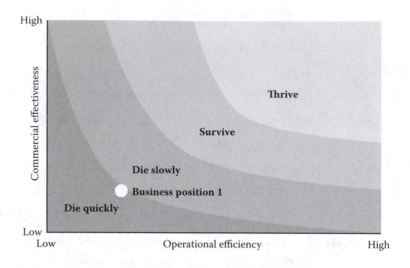

Figure 8.5   Business situation 1 – thrive or survive.

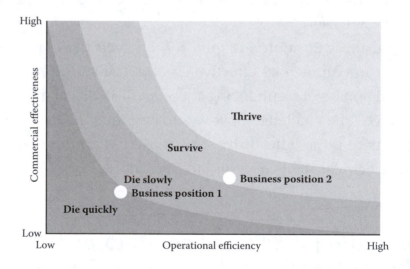

Figure 8.6   Business situation 2 – midway.

behind in terms of the basic operational capabilities of quality, cost, and delivery that one might expect. Therefore, at that time, there was a lot of emphasis placed on the elements "above the waterline," with the team using external and internal consultancy support

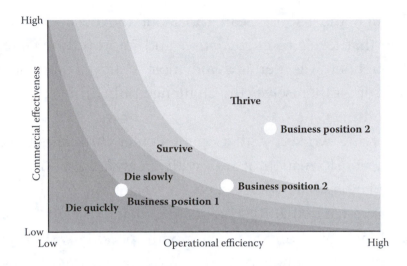

Figure 8.7 Business situation 3 – 2007.

to really drive visible performance improvement. After all, the business situation at the time was not good, and it was necessary to inject focus and pace to "get the ball rolling."

Two years in the business had made significant strides and a lot of the fundamentals were in place with much improved and stable processes that were tightly managed throughout. However, the business recognized that going forward, they wanted an improvement culture that was, in their own words, "self-propelling," and therefore Roadmap 2 focused more on the elements "below the waterline"—starting with deployed leadership through a series of development programs where individuals and teams were encouraged to "own" and drive the improvement culture.

Also, a lot of emphasis was placed on improving the strategy deployment systems, which resulted in the design and launch of the "Line of Sight" program. Of course, process improvements would also carry on through the use of Lean tools but the business realized that levels of *engagement* and improved *behavior* throughout was perhaps *the* most critical component and set for themselves the challenge of improving on all these fronts.

Having worked with Cogent Power throughout the Lean transformation, it was with great anticipation and trepidation that we revisited the plant for a progress review in March 2010. The business had basically "gone it alone" over an eighteen-month period, with only remote correspondence and infrequent meetings to discuss and share specific issues and potential ideas for further improvement. Moreover Marcel, Frans and Peter had all moved on and Cogent Power, that was part of the Corus Group, came under the ownership of Tata Steel, the Indian giant. Further, the market decline had resulted in a sharp drop in sales.

Here was the chance to see if the true meaning of the term "sustainable continuous improvement" was really in place. The term does not mean, "Has the business maintained the gains?" No, the term means much, much more than that. The visit would tell us whether or not the work we had done was enough to develop the capability, commitment, and indeed the culture needed to "continually improve the continuous improvement process." The findings were breathtaking.

Key Findings

First and foremost, what we saw was inspirational. Thinking back to where it had all started—the place, the look, the feel, the smell was different. This was indeed a very different place to be; it had pace and focus and smiling people. When asked, Greg (the Lean Manager) told us what he thought were the key phases of the journey, and his description is worth review in itself:

Roadmap	Phase	Description
1	Kaizen Blitz	Just getting it done
2	Learning to see	Look at the Value Stream Wastes and achieve business results time and time again
3	Shifting through the gears	Light the touch paper for everyone

Our first account of *Staying Lean* made reference up to and including Roadmap 2, but what were the key elements to move onward into Roadmap 3? That was the question that was answered through physical observations and the anecdotal stories from many members of the Cogent Power Team.

Did they "light the touch paper for everyone" through introducing rigorous systems of work or by developing behaviors among the workforces that would thrive on accountability and creativity? The answer, of course, was that they had done both and managing this paradox is a dilemma that I am sure many others are facing, and therefore looking at what Cogent Power has done may help.

Starting with Strategy Alignment, the design and implementation of the "line of sight" (LOS) process has clearly been instrumental. Out on the floor, there is an area "visible to most and accessible to all" where there is a working system for managing the Seven Key Performance Indicators for each of the Key Value Streams.

The Seven KPIs for value stream LOS are

1. Health and safety
2. OTIF
3. OEE
4. Scrap
5. Product rejects—customer and internal
6. Plant and process audits
7. WIP inventory

PLUS a review of the Ideas scheme by Value Stream
Each of the above had specific targets by value stream.

Nothing new there I suppose, but witnessing the weekly senior-level LOS meeting began to provide much more depth to the culture here. Attended by a small group of senior-level managers, the session was led by Ron (Operational Director) and each of the KPIs was reviewed in an intensely rigorous manner following a highly disciplined process.

Each KPI had its own board; each had a trend graph followed by at least two levels of Pareto analysis indicating clearly the reasons for the trend performance. This information was prepared by the value stream teams and line managers who, in turn, worked for the senior-level managers, who conducted the weekly review. Each and every board was interrogated and any issue was discussed through to root cause and agreed countermeasure with actions and owners established. If there was any significant issue and action needed to get the KPI back on track, then that KPI board was signaled with a large red plate at the top; this meant there would be further progress reviews conducted before the next week's LOS meeting.

A further development of the LOS process proved that Lean in Cogent Power was in fact "enterprisewide." The process witnessed on the shop floor was then replicated in the office areas around the visual management board, which had four critical KPIs focusing on purchasing, innovation, customer, and administration process performance and also included an office process audit system—now that was very impressive!

So here we have a system of management that has been developed and improved over time until it is now a recognized part of the landscape. The measures, targets, action plans, and visual management techniques have all been formed to make managing the business easier. Yet when I asked a few of the management team members to say what it is like to work here, the collective response was, "It's bloody hard." They talked about the pace, the rigor being relentless day after day, but also added how much they are enjoying working this way. Systems and procedures are one thing but adhering to such protocols is something else and often lets companies know when they are striving for a sustainable Lean culture.

> We are continuously building our commitment and capability to overcome obstacles, every single day. You know it's lean when it's getting harder and more fulfilling every day.
>
> —Greg, Lean Manager Canada

The next line of questioning was to determine how Cogent Power had developed its people and supported distributed leadership at all levels. As you would expect, there is not a single answer here but an aggregate of doing a number of small things continuously to develop people and align them to feel part of a Lean-thinking Team. During Roadmap 2, the business had introduced a set of "Lean behaviors" that were integrated into the HRM procedures with the purpose of making people understand what sort of behaviors were expected of them going forward. The behaviors included customer consciousness, enterprise thinking, collaboration, influence, taking initiative, innovation, and adaptation; and indeed, these behaviors were still reviewed as part of personal development plans for all employees. However, there had clearly been a focused effort on making accountability and ownership of continuous improvement the number-one discipline for everyone.

There has been an ongoing development program based on the key principles of accountability, with each defining the expected practices required to deliver on each. (see Connors, Smith, and Hickman, in *The Oz Principle: Getting Results through Individual and Organizational Accountability*)

Principle	Practice
SEE IT	Always obtain the perspectives of others.
OWN IT	Always ask, "What else can I do to help…?"
DO IT	Always focus on the vital few/top priorities.

Clearly, some posters and messages about this conveniently placed around a business will never be enough; but on further investigation, what became apparent was that the business was offering leadership support to help people become both capable and committed to the principles and practices of Lean Accountability.

In the Canadian plant a Lean Apprenticeship program has been introduced where employees from across the organization are invited to join the dedicated Lean Team for a six-month period. The selected Lean apprentices have come in from a range of operational and supporting disciplines, and work as a team of four for that time period. The business is now in the third year of this cyclic program and will soon have twenty-four Lean experts working back with their teams, leading and supporting continuous improvement activities as part of their full-time role. The approach appears to have really made a difference, especially when introducing new systems of applying continuous improvement.

One such example was the introduction of a Jidoka-type system where potential customer quality issues, when identified, would initiate an immediate stop on the line so the team could work on solving the problem. A process to do this was designed, trialed, and improved until the business was satisfied that this could and should be rolled out as standard best practice across all areas. This very visual system was christened "Jidoka/Blame-free problem solving at the line" and was launched with the hands-on help and support of the Lean Apprentices. When a Jidoka activity was needed, the apprentices would be on hand to facilitate problem solving and support the implementation of the solution. One of the apprentices (Todd) talked of his experience and learning here:

> To change someone's thinking at the workplace has been the hardest thing for me to learn. Jidoka was very difficult at first and it could easily take us one to two hours working through the problem as

most people were very uncomfortable with having to do this.

This had always been done for us by the management team but now stopping the line and asking the whole team to work together to put things right was a bit of a stretch, to say the least.

Now a typical Jidoka will take ten minutes, we have all become more comfortable with the expectation and more competent and confident of our problem-solving capabilities using the Jidoka process and toolkit.

The final piece of this ever-evolving jigsaw puzzle was to witness the time and effort and focus that the business has invested in training and development. The most obvious and visual aspect of this was that they have built the Training Centre, Lean Centre, and HR offices right in the middle of the operating plant. Here was a spot that was taken up with excess stock and poorly laid-out process lines just a few years earlier. This provided such as strong message to the workforce that this business is a team and everyone is in it together, which was most powerful. This is, after all, a steel processing plant and a noisy one at that, but even the LOS meetings were held at the workplace and managers at all levels could be seen by everyone, every day, working hard, taking care, and this was and remains a critical success factor.

The business has developed its very own Lean Learning Centre of Excellence, masterminded by Greg and Donna (the HR manager), and this program has been implemented and improved by the Team. The training program, although being "learning led," is very much focused on the people and team achieving actual business results. There are sixteen modules in total that cover classroom learning, hands-on tools, workshop kaizen activities, facilitation techniques, and leadership competencies. Certification is awarded based not simply on attendance but, more importantly, on an evidence-based report of improved business performance and personal learning.

Again, the Lean coaches and apprentices are on hand to support the learning events but possibly more importantly, the value stream and process managers identify the areas of improvement needed. This data comes from the LOS process where known issues and problems are addressed as part of the learning program.

Also linked to the LOS management process are a whole host of focused initiatives, including

■ Process Team competitions are launched to encourage and reward improvement activities, and these always have a focused theme and a focus (e.g., The OEE Competition/The Inventory Reduction Competition/The Health & Safety).
■ There is a comprehensive Ideas Scheme with process steps in place, each of which has targets that are reviewed to ensure that the system flows and is not too bureaucratic.
■ The Team has launched a very rigorous skills training program that is based on the tried and tested methodology of training within industry (TWI) with job instructions (JI) developed in a priority order based on issues and improvement needed on the Seven KPIs of the plant.

In Summary

We often hear people talk about the importance of "integration" but all too often it is difficult to see what this really is and how it really works. What really impressed us more than anything else at Cogent Power were the alignment, visibility, and integration of the systems and behaviors to deliver an improving business result.

Ron Harper, who clearly has played and still plays a pivotal role in continued progress of the business, summed it up with his three key steps for any improvement program:

Step 1 Align the strategic purpose and deployment processes to deliver value for your customers.

Step 2 Drive improvements across all the key business processes so all are aligned with providing value.

Step 3 Develop people in problem solving and work toward developing a culture of continuous improvement.

Observing the progress that had been made by the business led to a rethinking of the "Iceberg" model itself and how it could now represent what was taking place. The concept had started with an assertion that when you go into any organization, they tend to show you the physical aspects of continuous improvement, such as the Tools and Techniques for Process Management—that is, those elements that are visibly *above the waterline*. After Roadmap 2, our thinking went on to conclude that what really provided sustainability was developing the unseen elements *below the waterline*—that is, strategy and alignment, leadership, and engagement and behavior.

After this visit where we were provided insight into Roadmap 3, we began to see that in truly sustainable Lean organizations, the waterline actually drops and that all the elements become visible and integrated together (Figure 8.8). The strategy and alignment process of LOS was clearly visible; the leaders at all levels were where they needed to be, often at the Gemba; and people were engaged and aware of the importance of their behavior on others. What bound together these enabling elements were the rigorous applications of the tools and techniques that are so essential in effective process management.

The culmination of all this hard work and effort was recognized in 2009 when Cogent Power Canada won the AME Manufacturing Excellence Award for the Canadian region.

A Final Word

Addressing all elements of the iceberg helped to change the business, with the organization becoming much

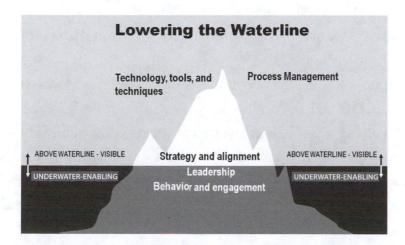

Figure 8.8   Lean Sustainability Iceberg Model at Roadmap 3.

more customer focused. The financial turnaround was accelerated by the exponential increase in sales that was achieved at controlled costs, and the business is now underpinned with the capability to "continuously improve the process of continuous improvement."

As Cogent Power in Canada became more customer focused, they changed the face of the company and moved up the value chain by taking on some processing for their customers. They were able to do this without adding extra internal costs due to the operational improvements they had made. In doing this, they were able to extend the supply chain out toward the customers.

The challenge now is to take the understanding and learning and achieve similar performance benefits across selected global supply chains, and to embed the changes for long-term sustainability.

At each stage of the Cogent Power journey there were lessons to be learned. For real, sustainable Lean, each element of the Lean Iceberg must be in place. If any element is missing, the whole is at risk. We try to summarize and illustrate this using a model for sustainable Lean change (Figure 8.9) adapted from the model developed by Ambrose (1987).

One of the key observations that we made was that organizational, or "double-loop," learning was taking place. The result was that improvements that could not have been envisaged at the start of the journey were now not only feasible, but also possible. Without organizational learning, many of the results would not have been achieved. We have illustrated the process that we observed by mirroring the Lean maturity path to McGill and Slocum's classification of organizational learning (Figure 8.10).

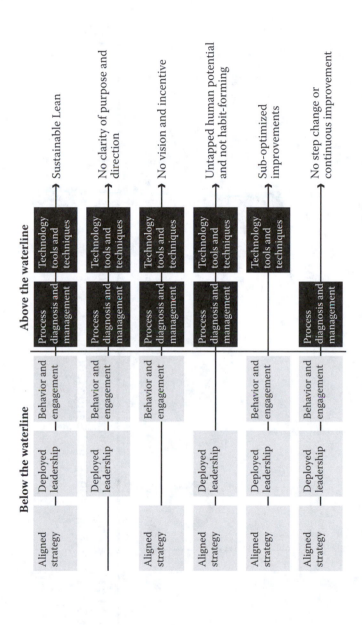

Figure 8.9 Sustainable Lean Change model (Based on Ambrose, 1987).

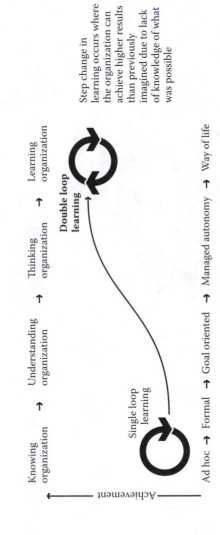

Figure 8.10   Lean maturity and organizational learning. Based on models by Bessant, Caffyn and Gallagher (2001), McGill and Slocum (1994), and Senge (2006).

See Peter Senge's book entitled *The Fifth Discipline: The Art and Practice of the Leaning organization* for more information on "double-loop" learning.

We believe that up until "Goal Oriented," the Lean journey is essentially deploying "Push Lean"; but when the step change occurs and the organization moves into "Managed Autonomy" and adopts double-loop learning, the journey takes on a different character and deploys "Pull Lean."

Following Cogent Power's Lean journey has shown that delivering sustainable Lean change is complex and not always achieved in a single journey. It requires focusing not only on the visible elements of Lean (i.e., process management, Lean tools, and techniques) but more importantly, on the invisible elements (i.e., strategy and alignment, leadership, and employee behavior and engagement). Real Lean leaders are people who are able to reflect and modify the route, recognizing that organizations need time to learn to be able to achieve the highest results; they know that it is only when they have learned that they are truly capable of "leading the Lean lifestyle."

Why don't you assess yourself, and your organization, against the Lean Iceberg? We call this *Action Learning* and we use an A3 form to do this (Figure 8.11). We have included a number of blank templates (see Figures 8.13a-e) for you to copy and use for your own diagnosis and learning; please feel free to use these in your organization.

As you embark on your Lean journey, we hope that this book helps you and gives you some insight into the issues that are involved. We wish you an enjoyable and rewarding experience.

ACTION LEARNING – Leading Lean

WHO: SITE: DATE:

SITUATIONAL PRESSURE FOR CI/CHANGE

What are the pressures faced in my role/area that require a need for continuous improvement change?

STRATEGY ALIGNMENT

What can I do personally to assist the process of strategy alignment and deployment for me and my team that will better enable CI?

LEAN LEADERSHIP

What do I need to do to better understand and adapt my style of leadership to best suit the CI challenge?

BEHAVIOR and ENGAGEMENT

What do I need to do to create an environment where people are engaged with CI and where their behavior drives CI as daily habit?

PROCESS DIAGNOSTICS AND MANAGEMENT

What do I need to do to ensure that myself and my team are able to diagnose process problems?

What do I need to do to ensure systems of corrective action and continuous improvement are in place and self-managing at the appropriate levels?

TECHNOLOGY, TOOLS AND TECHNIQUES

How do I select and apply the appropriate bundle of technology, tools and techniques for CI to make a positive impact to performance in my area?

PERSONAL ACTION PLAN

Do Now	Do Later
Priority 1	Priority 2

Figure 8.11   Action learning assessment.

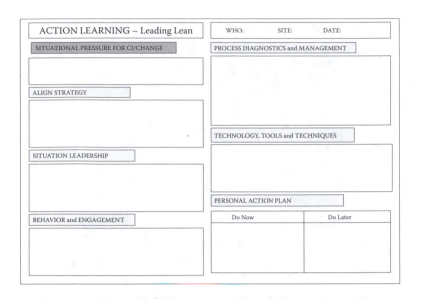

Figure 8.12   Blank template for your own action learning assessment.

- Assess how well is strategy aligned and deployed in your organization?

Strategy and Alignment at..	
What is done well?	**What is not done well?**
✳ ✳ ✳	✳ ✳ ✳
What could be done to improve?	**What is missing?**
✳ ✳ ✳	✳ ✳ ✳

Figure 8.13a   Blank template for your strategy and alignment assessment.

• Assess how good the leadership is in your organization?

Leadership at..	
What is done well?	**What is not done well?**
✳ ✳ ✳	✳ ✳ ✳
What could be done to improve?	**What is missing?**
✳ ✳ ✳	✳ ✳ ✳

Figure 8.13b   Blank template for your leadership assessment.

• Assess the levels of behavior and engagement in your organization?

Behavior and Engagement at..	
What is done well?	**What is not done well?**
✳ ✳ ✳	✳ ✳ ✳
What could be done to improve?	**What is missing?**
✳ ✳ ✳	✳ ✳ ✳

Figure 8.13c   Blank template for behavior and engagement assessment.

- Assess how well are processes managed in your organization?

Process Management at...	
What is done well?	**What is not done well?**
✳ ✳ ✳	✳ ✳ ✳
What could be done to improve?	**What is missing?**
✳ ✳ ✳	✳ ✳ ✳

Figure 8.13d   Blank template. For your process management assessment.

- Assess how well your organization uses tools, techniques and technology?

Tools, Techniques and Technologies at...	
What is done well?	**What is not done well?**
✳ ✳ ✳	✳ ✳ ✳
What could be done to improve?	**What is missing?**
✳ ✳ ✳	✳ ✳ ✳

Figure 8.13e   Blank template for your tools, techiniques and technology assessment.

Sources of Further Help

Research Assistance at Cardiff University

Cardiff University lean enterprise research centre (LERC) has a number of ongoing research programs in both the manufacturing and the service environments, on group and individual bases.

If you would like to discuss your specific requirement, please contact:

Dr. Pauline Found
Lean Enterprise Research Centre
Cardiff Business School
Cardiff University
Cardiff Business Technology Centre
Units 1.03–1.07
Senghennydd Road
Cardiff CF24 4AY, United Kingdom
e-mail: FoundPA1@cardiff.ac.uk or visit:
www.leanenterprise.org.uk or www.cuimrc.cf.ac.uk

Educational Assistance at Cardiff University

A range of educational courses are run at LERC, including Master's-level courses in Lean Operations for both Manufacturing and Service sectors. This is complemented by a number of open or bespoke short courses.

For further information, please contact:

Claire Gardner,
Education Manager
Lean Enterprise Research Centre
Cardiff Business School
Cardiff University
Cardiff Business Technology Centre
Units 1.03–1.07
Senghennydd Road
Cardiff CF24 4AY, United Kingdom
e-mail: gardnerca@cardiff.ac.uk or visit:
www.leanenterprise.org.uk

For further information on a range of bespoke consultancy and learning opportunities with S A Partners, please contact:

Information Desk
S A Partners
Business Development Centre
Pontypridd CF37 5UR, United Kingdom
e-mail: enquiries@sapartners.co.uk or visit
www.sapartners.com

LinkedIn Groups

Professor Peter Hines (http://www.linkedin.com/in/professorpeter-hines) leads a number of LinkedIn groups designed for those interested in creating a Lean enterprise in their organization. The groups provide a forum for discussion, debate, information exchange, as well as signposting to Lean enterprise events and activities. The groups are free to join and can be found at the following links:

Lean Enterprise Asia Pacific: http://www.linkedin.com/groups?gid=1819060

Lean Enterprise Benelux: http://www.linkedin.com/groups?gid=1842070

Lean Enterprise Canada: http://www.linkedin.com/groups?gid=2715139

Lean Enterprise Central and Eastern Europe: http://www.linkedin.com/groups?gid=1890400

Lean Enterprise Food and Drink: http://www.linkedin.com/groups?gid=1836371

Lean Enterprise Ireland: http://www.linkedin.com/groups?gid=1826782

Lean Enterprise Mediterranean: http://www.linkedin.com/groups?gid=1890317

Lean Enterprise Nordic: http://www.linkedin.com/groups?gid=1816278

Lean Enterprise Retail: http://www.linkedin.com/groups?gid=1836660

Lean Enterprise United Kingdom: http://www.linkedin.com/groups?gid=1801885

Lean and Green: http://www.linkedin.com/groups?gid=1826144

Recommended Publications

Companion Books to This Publication

Peter Hines, Ricardo Silvi, and Monica Bartolini, *Lean Profit Potential* (Lean Enterprise Research Centre, Cardiff, 2002). Available as a download from www.leanenterprise.org.uk. A practical guidebook on how to use Lean thinking to unlock hidden profit potential illustrated through application to a single car dealer.

Peter Hines and David Taylor, *Going Lean: A Guide to Implementation* (Lean Enterprise Research Centre, Cardiff, 2000). Available as a download from www.leanenterprise.org.uk. A practical introductory guidebook on how to go about starting to apply Lean thinking in a manufacturing environment.

Other Useful Texts

Icek Ajzen, *Attitudes, Personality, and Behavior* (The Dorsey Press, Chicago, 1988). The classic work on Theory of Planned Behavior.

D. Ambrose, (1987). *Managing Complex Change*. Pittsburg PA: The Enterprise Group Ltd.

B. M. Bass, *Leadership and Performance Beyond Expectation* (The Free Press, New York, 1985). Introduction to transformational leadership.

Jo Beale and Peter Hines, *Behavioral Aspects of a Sustainable Lean Manufacturing System* (Working Paper, Cardiff University Innovative Manufacturing Research Centre, Cardiff, 2007). An exploration of what you need to do to affect the behavior of people to make Lean implementations sustainable.

Warren Bennis, *On Becoming a Leader* (Perseus Publishing, Cambridge, MA, 2003). An excellent introduction to the difference between a manager and a leader.

John Bessant, Sarah Caffryn and Maeve Gallagher, (2000). An evolutionary model of continuous improvement behaviour. Technovation Vol. 21 pp. 67–77.

John Bicheno and Matthias Holweg, *The Lean Toolbox, 4th edition: The Essential Guide to Lean Transformation* (PICSIE Books, Buckingham, UK, 2009). An excellent guide to Lean transformations.

J. M. Burns, *Leadership* (Harper, New York, 1978).

Curt Coffman and Gabriel Gonzalez-Molina, *Follow This Path: How the World's Greatest Organizations Drive Growth through Unleashing Human Potential* (Random House Business Books, London, 2004). A worldwide survey on how engaged people are in their organizations and what can be done about it.

Jim Collins, *Good to Great* (HarperCollins, New York, 1991). A breakthrough text on the understanding how to be sustainable leader.

Roger Connors, Tom Smith, and Craig Hickman, *The Oz Principle: Getting Results through Individual and Organizational Accountability* (Penguin Group, London, 2004) ISBN 1-59184-024-4.

Stephen R. Covey and Rebecca Merrill, *The Speed of Trust: The One Thing that Changes Everything* (Simon and Schuster, New York, 2006).

Michael Cowley and Ellen Domb, *Beyond Strategic Vision: Effective Corporate Action with Hoshin Planning* (Butterworth-Heinemann, Oxford, UK, 1997). A must-read on Hoshin Planning.

Rick Delbridge, Lynda Gratton, Gerry Johnson, et al., *The Exceptional Manager: Making the Difference* (Oxford, 2007). Results of a collaborative research by Senior Fellows of the AIM initiative that focuses on the role of management in UK competitiveness.

Pascal Dennis, Andy *& Me: Crisis and Transformation on the Lean Journey* (Productivity Press, University Park, IL, 2005). An outline of the Toyota Production System and what it really means to apply it.

Pascal Dennis, *Getting the Right Things Done* (The Lean Enterprise Institute, Brookline, MA, 2006). A good summary of Strategy Deployment based around a case example.

George Eckes, *Making Six Sigma Last* (John Wiley & Sons, New York, 2001). A look at sustaining Six Sigma activities.

Bob Emiliani, *Real Lean—Understanding the Lean Management System* (The CLBM, LLC, Kensington, CT, 2007). A great insight into what it is and is not.

J. W. Gardner, *On Leadership* (Free Press, New York, 1990).

Eliyah Goldratt and Jeff Cox, *The Goal 2nd Edition* (Gower Publishing, Hampshire, UK, 1993). The definitive business novel.

R.D. Gordon, Conceptualizing leadership with respect to its historical-contextual antecedents to power, *The Leadership Quarterly,* 13(2), 151–167 2002.

P. Groon, Distributed leadership as a unit of analysis, *The Leadership Quarterly,* 13(4), 423–451, 2002.

Michael Hammer and Champney, J., *Reengineering the Corporation: A Manifesto for Business Revolution* (London, Harper Collins, 1993). Classic text on BPR.

Michael Hammer, in Joseph White, Next Big Thing, *Wall Street Journal,* November 26, 1996. A reflection on why BPR did not work and why a process view is necessary.

R. A. Heifetz and D. L. Laurie, The work of leadership, *Harvard Business Review,* Jan./Feb., 124–134, 1997.

Peter Hines and Nick Rich, Understanding improvement areas in the value stream. In Peter Hines, Richard Lamming, Dan Jones, Paul Cousins, and Nick Rich, *Value Stream Management*, pp. 13–31 (Pearson Education, London, 2000). A description of the use of a range of Value Stream Mapping tools.

Geert Hofstede and Gert Jan Hofstede, *Culture and Organizations: Software of the Mind, 2nd edition* (McGraw Hill, New York, 2005). Explores how organizational and national cultures differ, and how they can be managed.

Douglas Howardell, *Seven Lean Skills*, http://www.theacagroup.com/leanarticle.htm. An insightful text on developing leadership skills.

Spencer Johnson, *Who Moved My Cheese?* (Random House, London, 1999). A light-hearted approach to managing change.

J.R. Katzenbach & D. K. Smith, (1993). *The Wisdom of Teams: Creating the High-performance organization*. Boston: Harvard Business School.

John Kotter, *Leading Change* (Harvard Business School Press, Boston, 1996). A (or *the*) definitive text on change management.

John Kotter and Holger Rathgeber, *Our Iceberg is Melting: Changing and Succeeding under Any Circumstances* (Macmillan, Oxford, 2006). A light-hearted fable about doing well in an ever-changing world.

Kurt Lewin, Frontiers in group dynamics. In Cartwright, D., Ed., *Field Theory in Social Science* (Harper Brothers, New York, 1947).

Kurt Lewin, *Behavior and Development as a Function of the Total Situation* (Manual of Child Psychology, John Wiley & Sons, New York, 1946). Classic text on change management.

D. Lewis et al., Appreciative leadership: Defining effective leadership methods, *Organizational Development Journal,* 24(1), 87–100, 2006.

Jeffrey Liker, *Becoming Lean* (Free Press, New York, 1996).

Jeffrey Liker, *The Toyota Way: 14 Management Principles from the World's Greatest Manufacturer* (McGraw-Hill, New York, 2004). A classic text on the application of Lean thinking at Toyota.

Jeffrey Liker and David Meier, *The Toyota Way Fieldbook: A Practical Guide for Implementing Toyota 4Ps* (McGraw-Hill, New York, 2006). A step-by-step guide to developing a Toyota-style Lean enterprise.

Jeffrey Liker and Michael Hoseus, *Toyota Culture: The Heart and Soul of the Toyota Way*, (McGraw-Hill, New York, 2008). An in-depth examination of the "human systems" at Toyota.

John Lucey, Nicola Bateman, and Peter Hines, Achieving pace and sustainability in a major lean transition, *Management Services,* 48(9), 8, 2004.

John Lucey, Nicola Bateman, and Peter Hines, Why major lean transformations have not been sustained, *Management Services: Journal of the Institute of Management Services,* 49(2), 9–13, 2005. A brief, practical synopsis of why Lean efforts fail to be sustained.

John Lucey, Unpublished PhD Thesis, Cardiff, Wales, 2008.

David Mann, *Creating a Lean Culture* (Productivity Press, University Park, IL, 2005). Discussed standard work for leaders as part of a Lean management system.

Michael E. McGill and John W. Slocum Jr., *The Smarter Organization: How to Build a Business that Learns and Adapts to Marketplace Needs* (John Wiley & Sons, New York, 1994). A guide to transforming businesses into "smarter" organizations.

Yasuhiro Monden, *Toyota Production System* (Engineering and Management Press, Norcross, GA, 1988). Perhaps *the* definitive text on TPS.

Politis, J. D., Dispersed leadership predictor of the work environment for creativity and productivity, *European Journal of Innovation Management,* 8(2), 182–204, 2005.

Lyman Porter and Edward Lawler III, *Managerial Attitudes and Performance* (Irwin, Homewood, IL, 1968). An exploration of expectancy models and how these motivate people's behavior.

Nick Rich, *Total Productive Maintenance: The Lean Approach* (Liverpool Business Publishing, Liverpool, 2001). A useful companion book to guide the use of TPM.

Nick Rich, Nicola Bateman, Ann Esain, Lyn Massey, and Donna Samuel, *Lean Evolution: Lessons from the Workplace*, (Cambridge University Press, Cambridge, 2006). A detailed implementation guide and illustration of how other companies have applied Lean thinking in practice, highlighting the key challenges and pitfalls.

Mike Rother and John Shook, *Learning to See* (The Lean Enterprise Institute, Brookline, MA, 1998). Textbook summarizing how to use the Big Picture Mapping tool.

Edgar Schein, *Organizational Culture and Leadership* (John Wiley & Sons, New York, 2004). How to understand business culture and its link to leadership.

Peter Senge, *The Fifth Discipline: The Art and Practice of the Learning Organization*, *revised edition* (Random House Business Books, London, 2006). The classic text on developing a learning organization.

Samuel Smiles, *Self-Help* (Waking Lion Press, West Valley City, 2006). How to learn from mistakes.

Durward K. Sobek II and Art Smalley, *Understanding A3 Thinking* (Productivity Press, Boca Raton, FL, 2008).

David Taylor and David Brunt (Eds.), *Manufacturing Operations and Supply Chain Management—The Lean Approach* (International Thompson Business Press, London, 2000). A case book detailing the application of Lean thinking within an automotive supply chain context.

Victor Vroom, *Manage People, Not Personnel* (Harvard Business School Press, Boston, 1990). An exploration of expectancy models and how these motivate people's behavior.

James Womack and Daniel Jones, *Lean Thinking: Banish Waste and Create Wealth in Your Corporation* (Simon and Schuster, New York, 1996). The definitive text on the original five Lean principles and their application.

James Womack, Daniel Jones, and Daniel Roos, *The Machine that Changed the World* (Rawson Associates, New York, 1990). The classic Lean text that describes the results of benchmarking the world's major automakers.

Gary Yukl, An evaluation of conceptual weaknesses in transformational and charismatic leadership theories, in Groon, P., Distributed leadership as a unit of analysis, *The Leadership Quarterly,* 13(4), 423–451, 1999.

Jargonbuster

Big picture mapping: A specific visual approach designed to display at a high level a major part or whole *Lean enterprise.*

Catch-balling: The feedback and agreement process for plans with *policy deployment.*

Core processes: Those central processes that directly deliver results against targets. See also *key business processes, strategic processes, and support processes.*

Critical Success Factors (CSFs): Those key external or internal elements that a business needs to focus on for success, such as market growth or employee involvement.

Current State Map: A visual method of succinctly recording the key aspects of the current structure and processes in the whole or any part of a supply chain. See *big picture mapping.*

Flow: All activities being undertaken within the *Lean enterprise* at an even rate without delays, interruptions, or other batching.

Future State Map: A vision of a Lean system that is used as the guide for the change process.

Future Value-Adding (FVA) activity: Those activities within a company or supply chain that directly contribute to satisfying end consumers in some future time period and hence will be happy to pay for.

Hoshin Kanri: See policy deployment.

ILU charting: A skills and competency charting method that visually displays the existing position for each employee against a given set of targets to identify necessary training and development needs.

Key business process: Patterns of interconnected value-adding relationships designed to meet business goals and objectives, or the main cross-functional activities required in a business for success. See also *strategic processes, core processes,* and *support processes.*

Key Performance Indicators (KPIs): A set of measures designed to benchmark a business's most important characteristics against a set of strategic targets.

Lean: A consumer-focused approach to the provision of effective solutions involving the consumption of a minimum of resources.

Lean enterprise: The extended supply chain responsible for effectively satisfying consumer requirements using a minimum of resources.

Lean thinking: The process by which individuals can understand the need for, create, and implement a *Lean enterprise.*

Mapping: The use of appropriate tools and techniques to analyze the current situation in any process.

***Muda*:** The Japanese term for *waste.* Any activity that consumes resources but adds no value. A target for reduction or elimination.

Mura: The Japanese term for *unevenness.* Any activity that has not been leveled out, thus creating consequential complexity and cost. A target for reduction or elimination.

Muri: The Japanese term for *overburden.* Any activity that causes physical or mental stress to those people involved in it. A target for reduction or elimination.

Overall equipment effectiveness: A composite measure of the ability of a machine or process to carry out value-adding activity. OEE = % time machine available × % of maximum output achieved × % perfect output. It measures the degree to which machines are adding value by not being wastefully employed due to planned or unplanned downtime or in producing defects.

Pareto analysis: Sometimes referred to as the "80/20 rule." The tendency in many business situations for a small number of factors to account for a large proportion of events. For example, percent of total sales volume might be attributable to percent of customers and to percent of the product range. In terms of quality, percent of defects might be attributable to percent of causes. The percent is sometimes referred to as "the vital few."

Perfection: The complete elimination of *muda* so that all activities along a value stream create value.

Poke-yoke: A mistake-proofing device or procedure to prevent a defect during order intake or manufacturing.

Policy deployment: A strategic decision-making tool that focuses resources on the critical initiatives necessary to accomplish the *Critical Success Factors* of the firm. The term usually also encompasses the cascading of this by *key business process* together with the control, measurement, and feedback of results. Also known as *Hoshin Kanri*.

Profit potential: The effect on the "bottom line" of any activity that occurs during a Lean transformation program.

Pull: All activities being undertaken within the *Lean enterprise* according to and at the rate of the actual demand requirements of the end consumer.

Repeaters: Products or services that have an ongoing demand but are difficult to predict. They exhibit a medium risk to the business and may have medium levels of inventory. They generally have intermediate volumes but not dedicated facilities.

Runners: Products or services that have a regular, ongoing, predictable demand and that represent a low risk in the business and may have low inventories. Such products generally are high volume and have dedicated facilities.

Seven wastes: A framework of seven types of activity that do not add value, originally defined by the Toyota company.

Strangers: Products or services that are difficult to predict and will exhibit highly irregular but generally low demand profiles.

Support activity (SA) or necessary non-value-adding activity: Support activities that are necessary under the present operating system or equipment. They are likely to be difficult to remove in the short term but may be possible to eliminate in the medium term by changing equipment or processes.

Strategic processes: Those processes that help focus overall direction but do not have a direct impact on targets. See also *key business processes, core processes,* and *support processes.*

Support processes: Those processes only indirectly impacting on targets but providing support to the *core processes* that do. See also *key business processes, strategic processes,* and *core processes.*

Uptime: The percentage of time that a machine is available for productive work.

Value-adding (VA) activity: Those activities within a company or supply chain that directly contribute to satisfying end consumers, or those activities that consumers would be happy to pay for.

Value attribute: A value attribute is a feature directly desired by the customer and considered one of the core criteria in making a purchasing decision.

Value stream: The specific activities within a supply chain required to design, order, and provide a specific product or service.

Value stream mapping: The process of charting out or visually displaying a *value stream* so that improvement activity can be effectively planned. See *Mapping.*

Waste (W) or non-value-adding activities: Those activities within a company or supply chain that do not directly contribute to satisfying end consumers' requirements. It is useful to think of these as activities that consumers would not be happy to pay for. Sometimes called *muda.* See also *seven wastes.*

Index